GOOD TO GREAT LEADERSHIP:
Unleashing Your Transformative Leadership from Competence to Excellence

By Moe Nawaz

Publisher Information

Duke Brothers Ltd
1st Floor
One Mayfair Place
Mayfair
London E1J 8AJ
United Kingdom
Tel: +44 (0)207 516 1001

Copyright © 2022 Moe Nawaz

All rights reserved.

No part of this publication may be reproduced, stored, distributed, or transmitted in any form or by any means, electronic, mechanical, photocopying, recording, or otherwise, without prior written permission from the publisher, except for brief quotations used in reviews, commentary, or scholarly work as permitted under applicable copyright law.

This book is based on real-world experiences and engagements. In some cases, names, locations, industries, and identifying details have been changed to protect privacy. Any resemblance to actual persons or organisations is unintentional and coincidental.

Every effort has been made to ensure the accuracy of the information presented at the time of publication. However, neither the author nor the publisher assumes responsibility for any errors, omissions, or outcomes resulting from the application of the material contained herein. The strategies and examples provided are for educational and informational purposes only and should not be considered a substitute for professional advice, legal, financial, operational, or otherwise. Readers are solely responsible for complying with all applicable laws, regulations, and industry standards in their own jurisdictions.

No liability is accepted for any loss, damage, or disruption caused by the use or misuse of the content in this book.

For additional resources, mentorship, and strategic insights from **Moe Nawaz, The Strategic Architect**, please visit:

www.moenawaz.com

Acknowledgments

For those who shaped the architect, and strengthened the architecture.

My first acknowledgement is to God. Any clarity found in these pages did not originate with me. The design behind my life, its drift, its load, its failures, and its unexpected openings was never mine to claim. I have only tried to observe what was revealed and build accordingly, one quiet insight at a time.

To my family: you carried the invisible load that made this work possible. The late nights, the withdrawn weekends, the long silences that looked like absence but were actually thinking. If this book holds any structural integrity, it is because you held the structure around me.

To my mentors and teachers, Jay Abraham, Peter Drucker, W. Edwards Deming, Ray Dalio, Ben Gay III, Drayton Bird, and Eliyahu M. Goldratt: you offered discipline, not answers. You trained my attention toward structure rather than noise, toward cause rather than comfort, and toward clarity as an obligation rather than a preference. Your influence sits quietly beneath these pages.

To the leaders and organisations who allowed me into their most private rooms, from FTSE 100 and Fortune 500 boards to founders under pressure across Europe, the Middle East, Asia, and North America: this book was shaped inside those moments. Not the public rooms of presentation and performance, but the private ones where responsibility, uncertainty, and consequence coexist.

To the members of the Directors' WarRoom: your willingness to confront structural truth without spectacle continues to refine my thinking. Many of the patterns and observations in this book were forged through those conversations.

And to the reader: if you have chosen this work, you are already carrying weight. The fact that you are reading at all suggests you are building for continuity rather than adrenaline. The work begins here.

About The Author

Moe Nawaz, The Strategic Architect

Moe Nawaz works with leaders operating where decisions carry consequence and failure is costly. He is known as *The Strategic Architect*, not as a title, but as a function: identifying how work, decisions, accountability, and load actually move through organisations under pressure.

For more than four decades, Moe has advised FTSE 100 boards, high-growth founders, and institutional leaders across multiple continents. Much of this work is deliberately private. Its evidence is visible in organisations that stabilised, scaled, or endured moments they were not originally designed to withstand.

Where others focus on performance, Moe studies structure. Where behaviour is analysed, he traces load paths. Where success is celebrated, he looks for early signs of drift forming beneath it.

His work is anchored in the Five Strategic Pillars, Systemisation, Staffability, Scalability, Sustainability, and Sellability, understood not as tools, but as load-bearing conditions. Alongside them sits 3XV, not as a framework, but as cadence, the rhythm that determines whether organisational architecture holds or quietly degrades over time.

Moe's perspective was shaped through repeated exposure to structural reality. He has been removed from boardrooms for naming constraints too early, and later rehired when those constraints became unavoidable. Those experiences inform the spine of this book.

Today, Moe continues to work quietly with leaders facing complexity, scale, and irreversible decisions, helping them design organisations that no longer rely on personal heroics to function.

Table of Contents

Introduction **11**
   Why "Great" No Longer Lasts Good to Great Was Written for a Slower World.. 11
   When Excellence Becomes a Liability 14
   The Disappearance of "Great" Companies............................. 17
   The Question Leaders Now Face 20

PART I — The Fracture After Success **24**

  CHAPTER 1: When Performance Stops Scaling **25**
    Why Effort Plateaus Before Results.. 25
    Success as Structural Masking 28
    The First Signals Leaders Rationalise Away......................... 32
    When Leaders Become the Load-Bearing Structure 36

  PART II — The New Physics of Greatness, speed, AI, volatility **41**

  CHAPTER 2: Greatness Is Not A Structural Strategy **42**
    What Jim Collins Got Right, and What Time Exposed.......... 42
    Behaviour Scales Slower Than Complexity 45
    Why Many "Great" Companies Quietly Disappeared............ 49
    The False Comfort of Legacy Playbooks 53

PART III — From Leadership to Architecture, what carries weight.. **58**

  CHAPTER 3: Invisible Load And Organisational Blindness **59**
    Why Proximity Destroys Visibility 59
    Decision Congestion, Not Strategy, Slows Growth 63
    Why Internal Fixes Eventually Fail... 67
    The Cost of Waiting Until Pain Is Obvious............................ 71

PART IV — The Five Pillars, making greatness load-bearing 75

CHAPTER 4: When Structure, Not Effort, Becomes The Difference 76

The Shift from Performance to Capacity................................. 76
The Three Forces That Actually Carry Scale 80
Why Systems, Staffing, and Decisions Must Be Designed Together... 84
The Moment Leaders Stop Carrying the Organisation Personally 89

PART V: The Five Laws of Architectural Intelligence, how to see what you cannot see inside 93

CHAPTER 5 The Five Laws Leaders Must Obey 94

Law 1: Structure Reveals Truth Before People Do 94
Law 2: Load Always Transfers, It Never Disappears............. 98
Law 3: Complexity Always Outruns Culture 103
Law 4: The Bottleneck Is Usually a Decision, Not a Person 107
Law 5: Greatness Is Proven by Transferability 110

CHAPTER 6: The Greatness Audit, What to Measure Before You Move... 115

The 3XV Diagnostic, Clarity Test in One Page 115
Pillar Baselines, What "Strong" Actually Means 119
The Load Map, Where the Weight Is Really Sitting 123
The Drift Scan, Where "Fine" Is Quietly Becoming Fragile 128

CHAPTER 7 The 90-Day Rebuild Plan, Clarity, Capacity, Cadence.. 133

Days 1 to 15, Stop the Bleeding Without Cosmetic Change 133
Days 16 to 30, Decision Architecture Reset......................... 138
Days 31 to 60, Systemisation and Staffability as the First Load-Bearing Moves 142
Days 61 to 90, Cadence That Holds Under Pressure............ 146
The Moment the Organisation Feels Lighter........................ 150

CHAPTER 8 Staying Great, Preventing Drift, Protecting Optionality... 154

Why Greatness Decays, Even When Results Look Good 154

The Drift Prevention System, Signals, Cadence, Enforcement 158
AI as a Force Multiplier, Not a Crutch 163
Building Transferability, The Final Proof 168
CONCLUSION: Great Is Not a Status, It Is a Structure 174
The Choice Leaders Actually Make 178
A Final Warning, The Cost of Delay 182
A Final Warning, The Cost of Delay 187

Introduction

Why "Great" No Longer Lasts Good to Great Was Written for a Slower World

When *Good to Great* was first published in 2001, it landed with force for a reason.

The world it spoke to was stable enough for longitudinal studies, patient capital, and leadership behaviours to compound over time. Markets moved in cycles measured in years. Competitive advantages lasted long enough to be studied, codified, and replicated. Technology changed industries, but not overnight. AI was not compressing decision windows. Capital did not move at algorithmic speed.

In that world, the idea that disciplined leadership, the right people, and sustained focus could lift a company from "good" to "great" was not only persuasive, it was practical.

But that world no longer exists.

What has quietly changed is not leadership ambition or intelligence. It is **time, speed, and structural pressure**.

The half-life of advantage has collapsed.
Markets now reprice faster than organisations can adapt.
Information asymmetry has eroded.
Operational complexity has outpaced management bandwidth.

And leadership is carrying more load, across more dimensions, than at any point in modern business history.

The uncomfortable truth is this: many organisations today are not failing because they lack discipline, talent, or effort. They are failing because the **conditions that once allowed greatness to endure have disappeared**.

This is not a criticism of *Good to Great*.

It is a recognition of context.

The research behind the original work was rigorous. The insights were valid. But they were anchored in an era where:

- Structural drift happened slowly
- Decision latency was tolerable
- Scale did not automatically multiply fragility
- Leaders could personally compensate for missing structure

Today, those buffers are gone.

What used to be manageable friction has become structural drag.

What used to be leadership stretch has become leadership overload.

What used to be excellence has become exhaustion.

This explains a phenomenon many leaders quietly observe but rarely articulate:
the organisation looks successful on paper, yet feels increasingly heavy to run.

Revenue grows, but momentum feels brittle.

Headcount increases, but clarity decreases.

Meetings multiply, yet decisions slow.

xecution requires more effort for less leverage.

None of this would have surprised leaders in 2001.

But it would not have alarmed them either.

In a slower world, weight accumulated gradually. Leaders had time to adapt, redesign, and correct course. Today, weight compounds faster than reflection. Pressure rises before patterns are recognised. By the time symptoms are obvious, optionality has already narrowed.

This is why many of the companies once celebrated as "great" no longer exist in the form studied, and why many dominant organisations today will not exist in recognisable form a decade from now.

Not because the ideas were wrong.

But because **greatness without structural resilience does not survive acceleration**.

What *Good to Great* assumed, implicitly, was that leadership behaviour could remain ahead of organisational complexity. That assumption held when organisations were simpler, slower, and more forgiving.

It does not hold in an era where:

- AI compresses cycles of advantage
- Markets punish hesitation instantly
- Complexity scales faster than people
- Leaders are nodes inside systems they can no longer fully see

This creates a paradox modern leaders live inside every day.

They are more informed than ever.

More experienced than ever.

Surrounded by more data, advisors, dashboards, and reports than ever.

Yet many feel less certain.

Less able to see cause and effect.

Less confident that effort equals progress.

Less convinced that doubling down will work.

This book is written for that moment.

Not to discard the principles that once moved organisations from good to great, but to confront a reality those principles were never designed to handle: **a world where greatness decays unless the organisation itself is structurally capable of carrying it**.

The question is no longer how organisations become great.

The real question is why greatness no longer lasts.

And what must change, not in ambition or effort, but in how organisations are designed, interpreted, and carried forward under modern pressure.

That is the work this book begins.

When Excellence Becomes a Liability

For decades, excellence has been treated as the ultimate destination. Achieve it, codify it, protect it, and scale it. Boards reward it. Markets admire it. Careers are built on it. And for a long time, that logic held.

But something has quietly changed.

In today's environment, excellence is no longer a stable state. In many organisations, it has become a form of drag.

This is not because excellence is wrong, but because it is often **optimised for a world that no longer exists**.

Most organisations define excellence by what they have already mastered. Processes refined to near perfection. Leaders promoted because they embody what "good" looks like here. Metrics tuned to reward consistency, predictability, and repeatability. All sensible. All rational. All increasingly dangerous when the environment outside the organisation begins to move faster than the organisation itself.

Excellence hardens behaviour.

What once felt like discipline slowly becomes rigidity. What once looked like focus becomes selective blindness. Teams stop asking whether something still works and start defending the fact that it once did. Decision-making becomes precedent-driven rather than context-driven. The organisation does not consciously resist change, it simply cannot see it clearly enough to respond.

This is where excellence quietly turns into a liability.

High-performing organisations are especially vulnerable because they receive constant confirmation that their approach is correct. Customers still buy. Revenue still flows. People still execute. From the inside, there is no obvious signal that anything is wrong. The warning signs are subtle, delayed, and often misinterpreted as temporary noise rather than structural change.

The paradox is this:

The better you are at execution, the longer you can survive with misaligned structure.

Excellence extends the runway, but it also delays the reckoning.

Leaders inside successful organisations often sense this before they can articulate it. Results are still strong, but everything feels heavier. Decisions take longer. Coordination requires more effort. Meetings multiply. Reporting increases. Informal heroics become normalised to "keep standards high." The organisation is still performing, but it is no longer carrying its own weight cleanly.

This is not failure. It is load.

In many cases, excellence masks the early stages of structural mismatch. The organisation continues to win not because it is well designed for the current environment, but because capable people are compensating for what the structure no longer provides. Over time, that compensation becomes expected. Excellence turns into effort. Effort turns into exhaustion.

What makes this particularly dangerous is that excellence creates confidence. Leaders trust their judgement because it has been validated repeatedly. Systems are defended because they have delivered results. Culture is protected because it is associated with success. The organisation doubles down on what made it great, precisely when what made it great is becoming insufficient.

This is how decline begins without decline being visible.

In a slower world, excellence was a moat. In a faster, more volatile world, it can become an anchor. Not because standards are too high, but because they are calibrated to yesterday's conditions. The organisation is optimised for efficiency when adaptability is required. It is rewarded for consistency when responsiveness matters more.

The most dangerous moment is not when performance drops. It is when excellence still holds, but only through increasing strain.

At that point, leaders often reach for familiar solutions. More oversight. More process. More alignment meetings. More KPIs. All logical responses inside an excellence-driven system. And all of them add weight to a structure that is already struggling to carry its load

This book is not an argument against excellence.

It is an argument for recognising when excellence has outlived the environment it was designed for.

Greatness, in the modern context, is no longer about how well an organisation performs at what it already knows. It is about whether its structure allows it to see, adapt, and carry new forms of pressure without relying on ever-increasing effort.

That distinction is subtle. It is rarely taught. And it is almost impossible to recognise from inside the system once excellence has become part of the organisation's identity.

Which is why so many great organisations do not fail loudly.

They simply become heavier, slower, and less responsive, until the world moves on without them.

The Disappearance of "Great" Companies

When *Good to Great* was published in 2001, the assumption sitting quietly beneath the research was stability. Markets moved in cycles that could be studied over decades. Competitive advantages, once earned, could be defended. Time itself was a strategic ally.

That assumption no longer holds.

What has disappeared over the last two decades is not excellence, intelligence, or effort. What has disappeared is **longevity**. Greatness, as it was once defined, has become temporary. In many cases, it has become fragile.

This is not a moral judgement on leaders or organisations. It is a structural observation.

Since the early 2000s, a significant proportion of the world's largest and most admired companies have either vanished, merged under pressure, been dismantled, or slipped into long-term irrelevance. Some collapsed publicly. Others declined quietly. Many did not fail in a dramatic sense. They simply stopped mattering.

What matters is not the names themselves, but the pattern they reveal.

Historically, size and success created insulation. Capital strength, brand recognition, and market dominance bought time. Today, they often increase inertia. The very attributes that once protected organisations now slow them down. Scale amplifies structural weakness instead of absorbing it.

This is why the disappearance of great companies is rarely sudden. It is almost always **predictable in hindsight**.

The early signals are subtle. Decision cycles lengthen. Coordination costs rise. Senior leaders feel busier but less effective. Middle management adds layers to compensate for ambiguity. Reporting increases while clarity decreases. Performance is defended through effort, not structure.

From the inside, this looks like normal growing pains.

From the outside, it looks like architectural strain.

The critical mistake many organisations make is assuming that decline begins with poor performance. In reality, decline begins with **misalignment between load and design**. Performance often remains strong right up until the point where the organisation can no longer carry its own weight.

This is why so many once-great companies did not fail because they stopped doing the right things. They failed because the things they were doing no longer scaled structurally. What made them great became the very mechanism that limited their future.

Operational excellence hardened into rigidity. Cultural strength turned into resistance. Disciplined execution crowded out reflection. Success trained leaders to trust intuition longer than structure could support it.

None of this shows up clearly in financial statements. Revenue can grow while resilience declines. Profitability can mask brittleness. Market leadership can coexist with internal strain.

This is why data alone is insufficient.

If you look only at performance metrics, many disappearing companies looked healthy until very late in the cycle. If you look at organisational architecture, the warning signs appear much earlier.

Another misconception worth dismantling is the idea that disruption kills great companies. Disruption only finishes what structural weakness has already started. The real damage occurs long before the disruptor arrives.

New entrants move faster not because they are smarter, but because they carry less historical load. They are not weighed down by legacy processes, legacy incentives, or legacy assumptions. Their advantage is not innovation alone. It is **structural lightness**.

Large organisations often attempt to respond by borrowing the surface features of agility. They create innovation labs. They hire transformation leaders. They launch digital initiatives. They invest in technology. All of this can help, but none of it compensates for architectural mismatch.

You cannot out-innovate a structural problem.

This is where the conversation about greatness must change.

Greatness can no longer be defined solely by performance, culture, or leadership traits. Those elements still matter, but they are downstream. What determines whether greatness lasts is whether the organisation's **design can absorb pressure without distortion**.

The disappearance of great companies teaches us something uncomfortable but essential. Stability was never guaranteed. It was borrowed from a slower world.

In today's environment, speed does not merely increase competition. It compresses consequence. Small misalignments compound faster. Structural debt accumulates silently. By the time failure becomes visible, optionality has already collapsed.

This is why nostalgia is dangerous.

Revering past greatness without examining why it faded creates false confidence. It encourages leaders to replicate behaviours that no longer map to current conditions. It invites organisations to optimise for a world that no longer exists.

The lesson is not that greatness is impossible.

The lesson is that greatness without structural intelligence is temporary.

The organisations that endure are not those with the strongest leaders or the boldest visions alone. They are the ones that continually redesign themselves to match the load they are carrying and the velocity of the environment they operate in.

They treat success not as proof of correctness, but as a signal to re-examine structure.

They assume that what got them here is already becoming insufficient.

They do not wait for decline to justify change.

This shift in thinking is the foundation for everything that follows in this book. If greatness no longer lasts by default, then leadership must move upstream, away from heroics and toward design. Away from effort and toward architecture.

Only then does "good to great" become more than a moment in time.

The Question Leaders Now Face

At some point, every leadership team arrives at the same quiet crossroads. Not in a crisis. Not during collapse. Often at a moment when performance is still strong, margins are still acceptable, and the organisation is still being described, both internally and externally, as successful.

And yet, something has changed.

Decisions take longer than they used to. Alignment requires more explanation. Meetings multiply, but clarity does not. Results still arrive, but they arrive with more effort, more coordination, more personal involvement from the same small group of senior people. The organisation is moving, but it feels heavier.

This is the question leaders now face, whether they articulate it or not:

Are we still great, or are we simply compensating well?

In a slower world, this distinction mattered less. Time masked inefficiency. Human effort absorbed design flaws. Strong leaders could personally bridge gaps between teams, decisions, and priorities without paying an immediate price. The organisation might not have been well structured, but it was well carried.

That is no longer the environment leaders are operating in.

Speed has collapsed the margin for error. AI has compressed decision cycles. Markets punish hesitation faster than they reward brilliance. What once felt like excellence now behaves like drag. What once looked like control now reveals dependency. What once passed for leadership strength now quietly becomes organisational risk.

The uncomfortable truth is this: many organisations that still look great on the outside are already past the point where greatness is structurally supported.

They are running on leadership bandwidth rather than organisational capacity.

This is not a failure of intelligence. It is not a failure of commitment. It is not a failure of values or work ethic. It is the natural consequence of success outgrowing the structures that were originally designed to support it.

Most leaders, understandably, respond by doing what has always worked for them. They lean in harder. They add layers of oversight. They demand better reporting, tighter execution, more discipline.

They attend more meetings. They stay closer to decisions. They become the connective tissue holding the system together.

And for a while, this works.

In fact, it often works so well that it reinforces the behaviour. Performance holds. Problems stay contained. The organisation appears resilient. The leader feels indispensable. From the inside, it can feel like proof of competence.

From the outside, it looks like heroics.

The question leaders rarely stop to ask is whether this is strength, or whether it is structural debt being paid with human effort.

Because effort is not infinite. Attention does not scale. Judgement degrades under load. And the more a system relies on individual leaders to function, the more fragile it becomes, even as it appears stable.

This is where the meaning of "great" quietly shifts.

Greatness used to describe outcomes. Market position. Growth trajectories. Industry reputation. Shareholder returns. Those measures still matter, but they are no longer sufficient indicators of future viability.

The more relevant question now is whether greatness is carried by people, or by structure.

An organisation carried by people feels energetic but dependent. Remove one or two key individuals and the system strains. Decisions stall. Priorities blur. Momentum wobbles. Knowledge is concentrated. Authority is unclear. Accountability travels upward rather than outward.

An organisation carried by structure behaves differently. Decisions travel to where information lives. Authority is clear without being brittle. Teams move independently without fragmenting. Leaders create direction, not throughput. Pressure reveals issues early rather than catastrophically.

From the inside, both types of organisations can look successful. The difference only becomes obvious under sustained load, speed, or disruption.

This is why so many leaders are unsettled today without being able to explain why. Their experience tells them they are doing the right things. Their results tell them the organisation is still winning. But their intuition tells them something is misaligned.

That intuition is not fear. It is not doubt. It is not imposter syndrome.

It is architectural awareness.

It is the recognition, often subconscious at first, that the organisation is asking its leaders to do work that structure should be doing. That coordination is replacing clarity. That oversight is replacing design. That effort is replacing capacity.

The question leaders now face is not whether they are good enough to handle this.

It is whether handling it personally is the right answer at all.

Some leaders will continue as they are, increasing involvement, tightening control, carrying more weight. Many will succeed in the short term. Some will even be celebrated for it.

Others will pause long enough to ask a more difficult question.

Is our organisation great because it is well designed, or because we are working around its limitations?

That question, once asked honestly, cannot be unasked.

And it marks the true beginning of the journey from good to great in the world as it now exists.

PART I —
The Fracture After Success

CHAPTER 1:
When Performance Stops Scaling

Why Effort Plateaus Before Results

In the early stages of growth, effort and results appear tightly coupled. More hours produce more output. Extra focus delivers visible gains. Leaders learn, correctly, that energy matters. Teams respond. Progress feels earned.

This relationship does not break suddenly. It stretches.

As organisations grow, effort continues to scale linearly. Time, attention, meetings, oversight, reporting, coordination. All increase in proportion to ambition. Results, however, stop responding in kind. Output flattens. Momentum slows. The organisation works harder without moving faster.

This is the first plateau, and it is almost always misread.

Leaders interpret the slowdown as a signal about people. Motivation must be slipping. Standards need reinforcing. Accountability needs tightening. The instinctive response is to push harder, not to look differently. Effort becomes the lever because effort is the only variable still visible from inside the system.

What is rarely examined is capacity.

Effort is an input. Capacity is a design property. The two are not interchangeable.

Effort can be increased through will, pressure, incentives, or presence. Capacity can only be increased through structure. Once a system reaches its design limits, additional effort produces diminishing returns. Not because people are unwilling, but because the pathways through which work flows are saturated.

At this point, the organisation is no longer constrained by ambition or talent. It is constrained by architecture.

This distinction is uncomfortable because it removes the sense of control leaders are accustomed to. Effort is personal. Structure is impersonal. Effort feels actionable. Structure requires interpretation. As a result, most organisations stay in effort mode long after capacity has been exceeded.

The symptoms are familiar, especially to middle management.

Teams become busier but less effective. Work expands to fill available time, yet deadlines slip. Coordination consumes a growing share of energy. Decisions require more preparation, more alignment, more approval. Execution still happens, but it feels heavier. Progress depends on constant intervention.

From the inside, this looks like a productivity issue. From a structural perspective, it is saturation.

Systems do not scale the way people expect. They do not stretch elastically with demand. They have thresholds. Once crossed, flow degrades. Decisions queue. Exceptions multiply. Workarounds emerge. Informal processes replace formal ones. The organisation compensates, but at a cost.

Leaders often mistake this compensation for resilience.

Strong teams absorb the pressure. Capable managers bridge gaps. Experienced leaders step in to unblock issues personally. Results continue, reinforcing the belief that the approach is sound. In reality, the organisation is borrowing capacity from individuals to offset structural limits.

This borrowing is invisible in performance metrics. Revenue can grow while capacity declines. Headcount can increase while throughput stalls. The organisation appears healthy because people are carrying weight that the system no longer can.

The first plateau is rarely recognised as a structural signal because it does not feel like failure. It feels like friction. Manageable friction. The kind that can be overcome with effort, at least for a while.

This is where the confusion between energy and capacity becomes dangerous.

Energy can push output temporarily above sustainable levels. Capacity determines what can be carried repeatedly without distortion. When leaders rely on energy to solve capacity problems, they create a system that only functions under strain.

Middle managers experience this first. They are closest to the work and furthest from redesign authority. They feel the drag before it is visible at the top. Targets are technically achievable, but only through constant adjustment. Plans hold only if nothing unexpected occurs. Success depends on knowing who to call, not on how the system works.

This is not a morale problem. It is not a skills gap. It is not a lack of discipline.

It is structural saturation.

Performance stalls not because people weaken, but because the organisation has reached the limits of what its current design can carry. Additional effort does not fail immediately. It simply stops compounding. The return on energy declines. Each unit of progress costs more attention, more coordination, more exception handling.

Leaders who have succeeded through effort often struggle most at this point. Their experience tells them that leaning in works. Their track record confirms it. The plateau feels like resistance, not a warning. Pushing harder feels responsible.

What is actually happening is quieter.

The system is signalling that it cannot scale further without redesign. The signal is not delivered as a breakdown. It arrives as fatigue, congestion, and diminishing leverage. It is easy to explain away. Easy to rationalise. Easy to attribute to temporary conditions.

The cost of misreading this moment is not immediate failure. It is delay.

Delay allows structural debt to accumulate. Workarounds harden. Informal dependencies become permanent. Leaders become load-bearing components. By the time results visibly decline, the organisation has already lost optionality.

The first plateau is the last moment where change is cheap.

After that, effort still works, but only as a substitute for structure. And substitutes always cost more than design.

This is why competence fails under growth. Not because competence disappears, but because competence alone cannot expand capacity. Once the system saturates, excellence becomes effort, and effort becomes the constraint.

The organisation has not stopped performing. It has stopped scaling.

Success as Structural Masking

Success is rarely neutral. It does not simply reward what works. It also conceals what does not.

In the early and middle phases of growth, positive results act as a form of insulation. Revenue increases. Customers stay. Markets respond. From the outside, the organisation appears healthy. From the inside, success creates a powerful signal that the underlying design must be sound.

This is the moment where structural weaknesses are most effectively hidden.

Early wins compensate for weak architecture. Strong performance absorbs friction that would otherwise demand attention. Gaps in decision flow are bridged informally. Ambiguities in accountability are resolved through personal relationships. Incomplete systems are carried by capable individuals who know how to make things work despite the design.

Nothing breaks because people intervene.

This is why success delays corrective action. The organisation is not rewarded for being well designed. It is rewarded for delivering outcomes. As long as outcomes arrive, the cost of how they arrive remains largely invisible.

Strong people play a central role in this masking.

High performers adapt instinctively. They anticipate problems before they surface. They step outside formal roles to protect delivery. They escalate selectively. They absorb complexity rather than expose it. Over time, this behaviour becomes normalised. The organisation comes to rely on individuals who can compensate for what the structure does not provide.

From a leadership perspective, this looks like strength.

Teams are resilient. Managers are proactive. Leaders feel supported by people who can handle ambiguity. The system appears flexible. In reality, flexibility is being simulated through effort.

Weak systems are rarely exposed when strong people are present. They are only exposed when those people leave, burn out, or become overwhelmed. Until then, the organisation mistakes personal competence for structural adequacy.

Revenue growth amplifies this illusion.

As revenue increases, complexity increases with it. More customers introduce more variation. More products add more dependencies.

More markets create more exceptions. Each layer of growth adds load to decision-making, coordination, and prioritisation.

If the architecture does not evolve at the same rate, decision congestion begins to form. Approvals stack. Meetings multiply. Escalations increase. None of this appears in headline performance metrics. Revenue can grow while flow degrades.

From the boardroom, this looks like healthy expansion. From the middle of the organisation, it feels like drag.

The danger is not complexity itself. Complexity is a natural consequence of growth. The danger is unmanaged complexity. Complexity that accumulates without corresponding redesign. Complexity that is carried by people instead of structure.

During good years, this accumulation is almost impossible to see clearly.

Success creates narrative momentum. Positive results encourage leaders to protect what appears to be working. Processes are left intact because they have delivered outcomes. Decision rights remain ambiguous because they have not caused visible failure. Informal workarounds are tolerated because they are effective.

The organisation does not pause to ask whether success is being produced efficiently, or sustainably. It asks only whether success is being produced.

This is structural masking.

The architecture is not tested under neutral conditions. It is tested under pressure. Success reduces perceived pressure. As a result, the organisation continues to operate beyond its design limits without recognising the cost.

One of the most common signs of this masking is the normalisation of heroics.

Late nights become routine. Escalations become expected. Senior leaders stay close to execution. Middle managers spend more time coordinating than improving. Everyone is busy. Everyone is committed. Performance holds.

From the inside, this feels like dedication. From a structural perspective, it is compensation.

Another sign is the gradual shift in how decisions are made. As complexity increases, decisions that were once distributed begin to travel upward. Leaders become involved not because they want control, but because the system does not provide clear resolution pathways. Each escalation feels reasonable in isolation. Collectively, they create congestion.

Revenue growth disguises this congestion because outcomes still arrive. The delay is not in delivery, but in leverage. Each decision takes longer. Each initiative requires more alignment. Each problem consumes more senior attention. The organisation moves, but with increasing effort.

Success convinces leaders that these costs are acceptable.

It is important to be precise here. This is not denial. It is not arrogance. It is not complacency. It is pattern recognition based on past experience. Leaders who have built successful organisations have learned that persistence works. They have evidence. The system has responded before.

What changes is not leadership quality, but context.

In a slower environment, the lag between structural strain and visible failure was long. Leaders had time to notice, adjust, and redesign. In a faster environment, that lag compresses. Structural debt accumulates quickly. By the time strain becomes undeniable, options are already limited.

Success, in this sense, is not a reward. It is a delay mechanism.

It postpones exposure by allowing the organisation to continue operating through effort. It validates behaviours that should have triggered redesign. It reinforces confidence in approaches that are becoming misaligned with scale.

This is why many leaders feel unsettled during periods of strong performance. The numbers look right, but the experience feels wrong. The organisation is winning, but it is harder to run. The weight is increasing, even as results remain positive.

That discomfort is often suppressed because success does not invite doubt. It invites protection.

The critical point is this: success does not validate design. It only postpones exposure.

Every organisation eventually encounters conditions that its architecture cannot absorb. The question is whether that encounter happens early, when redesign is cheap, or late, when intervention is disruptive and costly.

Success pushes that encounter further into the future. It does not remove it.

Understanding this is not an indictment of past decisions. It is a recognition of how systems behave under growth. Strong results are not proof of structural health. They are simply proof that the organisation has not yet been fully tested.

This is the fracture after success. Not collapse, but concealment. Not failure, but delay.

And delay is where most of the damage quietly accumulates.

The First Signals Leaders Rationalise Away

Structural strain rarely announces itself as a problem. It arrives as interpretation.

Before results stall, before customers complain, before margins tighten, the organisation begins to behave differently. The signals are subtle, individually reasonable, and easy to explain. None of them feel like warnings at the time. Together, they form a pattern that is almost always recognised too late.

The first signal is decision speed.

Decisions that once moved quickly begin to slow. Not dramatically, just perceptibly. More context is requested. More voices are included. More scenarios are explored. From the inside, this feels responsible. Leaders describe it as being thoughtful, prudent, or risk-aware. In complex environments, caution appears sensible.

What is actually happening is congestion.

As load increases, decisions encounter more dependencies. Authority becomes less clear. Information is fragmented across functions. To compensate, decisions travel upward or sideways in search of certainty. Each additional step feels justified. The slowdown is framed as maturity rather than friction.

The second signal is the multiplication of meetings.

Meetings increase in frequency and duration. New forums are created to coordinate across teams. Standing updates become regular. Alignment sessions are scheduled to ensure everyone is on the same page. From a leadership perspective, this looks like good governance. Communication improves. Visibility increases.

In reality, meetings are absorbing the work that structure is failing to do.

When decision rights are unclear, meetings substitute for clarity. When priorities conflict, discussion replaces resolution. When accountability is diffuse, consensus becomes the default. None of this feels wrong in isolation. Each meeting has a purpose. The issue is cumulative load.

The organisation begins to spend more time talking about work than doing it, not because people are inefficient, but because flow is breaking down.

The third signal is duplication.

Multiple teams begin working on similar problems. Parallel analyses appear. Different versions of the same report circulate. Processes are double-checked. Outputs are reviewed by more than one group. This is usually justified as checks and balances. In regulated or high-risk environments, redundancy feels prudent.

Duplication, however, is rarely designed deliberately. It emerges when trust in the system erodes.

When outcomes are uncertain, people protect themselves by adding layers. They create backups. They verify independently. They hold their own versions of the truth. This behaviour is not wasteful by intention. It is adaptive.

From the inside, duplication feels like diligence. From a structural perspective, it is a signal that flow is no longer reliable.

The fourth signal is escalation.

Issues that were once resolved locally begin to travel upward. Managers involve senior leaders earlier. Decisions are deferred pending approval. Exceptions become common. Leaders are asked to weigh in on matters that should not require their attention. This is often framed positively as leadership visibility or support.

Leaders respond because they care. They unblock issues. They provide direction. They restore momentum. The organisation learns that escalation works.

Over time, escalation becomes normalised.

What started as support becomes dependency. Leaders become part of the operational flow rather than the designers of it. The system adjusts around their availability. Decisions wait for presence. Progress slows in their absence.

None of this feels negligent. It feels responsible.

Each signal, taken alone, can be explained rationally. Slower decisions reflect complexity. More meetings improve alignment. Duplication reduces risk. Escalation ensures quality. Leaders are not wrong to accept these explanations. They align with experience and values.

The problem is not the explanation. It is what is being explained away.

These signals are not causes. They are symptoms. They indicate that the organisation is compensating for structural strain through behaviour. People are adapting intelligently to a system that no longer carries load cleanly.

The rationalisation happens because success has trained leaders to trust their judgement. The organisation is still performing. Customers are still served. Targets are still met. The cost of these adaptations is not immediately visible. It shows up as effort, not failure.

This is why the early signals are so dangerous.

They do not trigger alarm. They trigger interpretation. Leaders explain them as natural consequences of growth. Temporary adjustments. Signs of professionalism. The organisation adapts, and adaptation is rewarded.

What is not questioned is whether these adaptations are sustainable.

As these behaviours accumulate, they change the character of the organisation. Decision speed declines without an obvious bottleneck. Meetings crowd calendars without improving clarity. Duplication consumes capacity without increasing confidence. Escalation concentrates load at the top.

The organisation still moves, but it moves differently. Progress depends less on design and more on coordination. Outcomes depend more on individuals and less on systems. The organisation becomes more fragile even as it appears more controlled.

This is inevitability, not error.

No leader chooses this path deliberately. It emerges from the interaction between growth, complexity, and success. The organisation does what it must to keep performing. People adjust. Leaders support. Results hold.

By the time these signals are recognised as structural warnings rather than operational quirks, they are deeply embedded. Removing them feels risky. The organisation has learned to rely on them.

This is why early intervention is rare.

There is no single moment that demands it. No obvious failure. No clear line where caution becomes congestion or support becomes dependency. The shift is gradual. Each step makes sense. Each rationalisation is defensible.

The first signals leaders rationalise away are not mistakes. They are adaptations to unseen limits.

Recognising them requires stepping outside the system that produced them. From within, they feel like maturity. From above, they reveal saturation.

This is the quiet accumulation that precedes the fracture. Not because leaders ignored the signs, but because the signs did not look like signs at all.

When Leaders Become the Load-Bearing Structure

There is a moment in the life of most successful organisations when leadership changes shape.

It is not announced. It is not planned. It does not arrive with a title change or a formal redesign. It emerges quietly, through accumulation. Leaders begin to carry weight that the organisation itself no longer can.

At first, this feels like involvement.

Leaders stay close to decisions to maintain standards. They attend more meetings to ensure alignment. They step in to unblock issues because it is faster than waiting for resolution. None of this appears excessive. It looks like responsibility. It looks like care.

What is happening structurally is different.

Decisions that should be resolved by clear authority paths are being absorbed by individuals. Exceptions that should be handled by design are escalated to judgement. Ambiguity that should be eliminated through structure is managed through presence.

Leadership becomes the system.

This is the quiet shift from leadership to shock absorber.

A shock absorber does not remove force. It dampens it. It prevents visible damage by absorbing impact repeatedly. Over time, the system learns to rely on it. The absorber wears down, but the structure around it remains unchanged.

In organisations, leaders begin to perform this function without realising it. They absorb conflict between priorities. They reconcile misaligned incentives. They resolve gaps between functions. They carry context that the organisation cannot transmit on its own.

Because they are capable, this works.

Heroic reliability is rewarded. The leader who can always be counted on becomes indispensable. The organisation stabilises around them. Performance holds. From the outside, nothing appears wrong.

From a structural perspective, dependency is forming.

When leaders absorb decisions meant for systems, those systems never mature. Decision rights remain unclear because escalation works. Processes remain incomplete because judgement fills the gaps. Accountability remains fuzzy because leaders intervene before failure forces clarity.

The organisation does not experience the full consequence of poor design. It experiences relief.

This relief is deceptive.

Each time a leader steps in, they reduce immediate friction while increasing long-term load. The system adapts by routing more weight through the same individual. Over time, this becomes normalised. People learn where to go to get things done. Progress is no longer a function of structure, but of access.

This is not about ego or control. In most cases, leaders do not seek this role. They inherit it. They respond to what the organisation requires to keep moving. Their presence becomes a substitute for design.

The cost of this substitution is largely invisible at first.

Leaders become busier, but not necessarily more effective. Their calendars fill with issues that should not require their attention. Decision quality begins to vary with availability. Strategic thinking is squeezed between operational demands. Fatigue increases, but performance still holds.

Downstream, the organisation adapts again.

Middle managers escalate sooner. Teams wait for confirmation before acting. Initiative narrows. Risk is deferred upward. The organisation becomes cautious, not because people lack confidence, but because authority is unclear.

This creates an invisible tax.

Time is spent preparing leaders for decisions they should not need to make. Meetings are scheduled to secure alignment that should be embedded in structure. Work slows at handoff points. Energy is consumed managing uncertainty rather than producing value.

None of this appears in performance dashboards. It appears in experience.

The organisation feels heavier. Progress requires more coordination. Momentum depends on the same few individuals. When those individuals are absent, decisions stall. When they are present, throughput increases.

This variability is not a leadership strength. It is a structural weakness being masked by competence.

As this pattern deepens, leaders often feel conflicted. Their involvement is clearly helping. Removing themselves feels irresponsible. Delegation appears risky because the system does not reliably support it. The organisation seems to need them.

This is the trap.

The more leaders compensate for structural gaps, the harder it becomes to see those gaps clearly. The organisation stabilises around their intervention. Redesign is postponed because things are working. The system never experiences enough strain to force change, because leaders are absorbing it.

Over time, the role of leadership quietly inverts.

Instead of designing the organisation to carry load, leaders carry the organisation. Instead of creating capacity, they become capacity. Instead of enabling flow, they manage friction.

This is not sustainable, but it is durable enough to persist for years.

The danger is not burnout, although that often follows. The deeper danger is fragility. When leadership becomes load-bearing, the organisation's ability to function independently erodes. Succession becomes risky. Scale becomes harder. Optionality shrinks.

Greatness, in this state, is performative.

It depends on specific people being present, engaged, and available. Remove them, and the system struggles. Keep them, and the system never learns to stand on its own.

This is the point where competence finally fails under growth.

Not because leaders are no longer capable, but because their capability has become the constraint. The organisation has reached a size and complexity where it can no longer be carried by individuals, no matter how strong.

This section matters because it sets the boundary for everything that follows.

If leaders are still the load-bearing structure, no amount of vision, strategy, or effort will produce durable greatness. The organisation will continue to perform, but it will not become structurally resilient.

Until leadership load is designed out of the system, greatness remains conditional.

And conditions, under pressure, eventually break.

PART II —
The New Physics of Greatness, speed, AI, volatility

CHAPTER 2:
Greatness Is Not A Structural Strategy

What Jim Collins Got Right, and What Time Exposed

Good to Great earned its influence because it described a real phenomenon, observed carefully, in a world where the conditions allowed it to hold. The discipline it championed was not theoretical. The focus was not decorative. The emphasis on leadership humility and long term commitment reflected what successful organisations actually needed at the time.

That deserves acknowledgement.

The companies studied were operating in markets where advantage could be sustained long enough to be examined. Feedback loops moved slowly. Strategy had time to settle. Execution could compound without being constantly disrupted. In that environment, behavioural excellence mattered enormously. Leaders who were disciplined, patient, and restrained outperformed those who chased novelty or overreached.

Behaviour was a lever because behaviour could stay ahead of complexity.

What Good to Great captured accurately was that success was not driven by charisma or bold vision alone. It came from consistency. From saying no. From aligning people around a clear direction and sticking with it. In a relatively stable context, those traits translated directly into performance.

The research was sound. The conclusions were reasonable. The book became influential because it matched lived experience.

What time has exposed is not a flaw in the thinking, but a shift in the environment that the thinking relied on.

Behavioural excellence assumes that the system within which behaviour operates is relatively forgiving. It assumes that strong leadership habits can compensate for imperfections in design. It assumes that the pace of change allows leaders to observe, interpret, and adjust before consequences compound.

Those assumptions held when markets moved slowly enough for leaders to stay ahead of the organisation's own complexity.

They do not hold now.

The most important change is not technological, although technology has accelerated it. It is temporal. The half life of advantage has collapsed. Feedback arrives faster. Pressure accumulates sooner. Misalignment is punished quickly. Organisations no longer have the luxury of learning slowly from small mistakes.

In that context, behavioural excellence is still valuable, but it is no longer sufficient.

Discipline cannot absorb volume. Focus cannot resolve congestion. Humility does not redesign decision flow. Leadership traits operate within a structure. When that structure saturates, the effectiveness of even the best behaviours declines.

This is where time exposed a limitation that was not visible in the original work.

Slower feedback loops masked structural weakness. Organisations could carry hidden inefficiencies for years without visible consequence. Strong leaders could personally compensate. Systems that were not well designed could still perform because the environment allowed margin for error.

That margin has largely disappeared.

Today, complexity scales faster than behaviour. Organisations add products, markets, partners, technologies, and regulatory obligations at a pace that outstrips the ability of individuals to coordinate them intuitively. What once felt manageable now feels heavy much earlier in the growth curve.

In the past, leaders could rely on judgement to bridge gaps. Now, those gaps multiply faster than judgement can cover them.

This is not a critique of the leaders Collins described. It is a recognition that the conditions that allowed them to succeed are no longer stable. Behavioural excellence did not fail. The environment changed.

Another important distinction is that Good to Great focused on what leaders did. It assumed that if leaders behaved correctly, the organisation would follow. That assumption holds when the organisation is simple enough for leadership behaviour to propagate cleanly.

As organisations grow larger, more distributed, and more interdependent, behaviour no longer travels far enough on its own. Signals distort. Intent degrades. Decisions bottleneck. The organisation becomes less responsive to leadership example, not because people are disengaged, but because the system is too complex to be carried by behaviour alone.

In a slower world, leadership behaviour could remain ahead of organisational complexity. In a faster world, complexity outruns it.

This is why many modern leaders recognise the principles of Good to Great intellectually, yet struggle to apply them meaningfully. They attempt to increase discipline, sharpen focus, reinforce values, and model humility. They do the right things. The organisation responds, but only partially.

The gap is not effort. It is architecture.

Good to Great did not fail because its ideas were wrong. It became incomplete because it assumed a world where greatness could be sustained through behaviour without continuous redesign. Time has shown that assumption to be fragile.

The respectful conclusion is this.

Behavioural excellence is a necessary condition for greatness, but it is no longer a sufficient one. Without structural intelligence, discipline turns into rigidity. Focus becomes narrowness. Humility becomes hesitation. The very traits that once produced greatness can slow adaptation under accelerated pressure.

What time exposed is not the end of Good to Great, but its boundary.

Beyond that boundary, leadership must move upstream, away from traits and toward design. Away from personal excellence and toward organisational capacity. Away from what leaders do, and toward what the organisation can carry without them.

That is the shift this book now makes, not in opposition to the past, but in response to the present.

Behaviour Scales Slower Than Complexity

Leadership behaviour has limits.

This is not a judgement on its importance. It is a recognition of scale. Behaviour operates through people. Complexity accumulates through systems. The two expand at different rates.

In small or moderately sized organisations, leadership habits travel far. Clear expectations shape decisions. Cultural norms guide behaviour. Leaders can model standards and see them reflected quickly. The organisation remains legible. Cause and effect are close enough to be felt.

As organisations grow, this relationship changes.

Volume increases. Interfaces multiply. Decisions span functions, geographies, technologies, and time zones. Information fragments. Dependencies increase. The distance between intent and outcome lengthens. Behaviour does not degrade, but its reach does.

Habits do not absorb volume.

A leader can be disciplined, focused, and consistent, yet still preside over an organisation where work queues, approvals stack, and decisions stall. The behaviour is sound. The system is saturated. No amount of personal discipline can eliminate congestion created by unclear decision rights or poorly designed flow.

This is where leaders often experience a sense of paradox. They are doing the right things more rigorously than ever, yet results feel harder to produce. The organisation is committed, but slow. Standards are high, but execution strains.

The instinctive response is to reinforce behaviour.

More emphasis on accountability. Clearer expectations. Stronger cultural messaging. These interventions feel appropriate because behaviour is visible and controllable. Structure, by contrast, is diffuse and harder to diagnose.

The problem is that behaviour cannot resolve structural constraints.

Culture does not resolve decision congestion. It can influence how people behave within decisions, but it cannot determine where decisions should sit, how they should flow, or how many must be made. When authority is unclear, culture fills the gap temporarily, often by deferring upward or seeking consensus. Over time, this creates delay.

Excellence, in this context, amplifies strain.

High standards increase workload. Thoroughness adds steps. Caution introduces checks. Pride in quality leads to review. When structure lags behind complexity, excellence multiplies the pressure on the system. What once produced superior outcomes now produces drag.

This is not a failure of excellence. It is a mismatch.

Behavioural excellence assumes that the system can carry the weight it generates. When it cannot, excellence becomes effort intensive. The organisation works harder to maintain standards that the architecture no longer supports efficiently.

This is why many high performing organisations feel heavy long before they fail.

The people are capable. The culture is strong. Leadership is competent. Yet throughput slows. Decision speed declines. Coordination costs rise. The organisation is not underperforming. It is overburdened.

The root cause is not a lack of commitment. It is the exponential nature of complexity.

Each additional product, market, regulation, technology, or partnership adds more than incremental load. It adds interaction effects. Decisions intersect. Exceptions proliferate. Dependencies multiply. The system's complexity grows faster than headcount, faster than leadership bandwidth, faster than behavioural reinforcement.

Behaviour scales linearly. Complexity scales exponentially.

This gap is where modern organisations get trapped.

Leaders double down on what they can control. They reinforce values. They clarify vision. They model discipline. These actions still matter, but they no longer move the system proportionally. The organisation absorbs the intent, but the structure cannot transmit it cleanly.

The result is frustration without obvious failure.

Leaders sense that something is wrong, but the usual levers no longer produce the expected outcomes. They have evidence that behaviour worked in the past. They have no clear signal that it has stopped working. The degradation is gradual.

Middle managers feel this acutely. They translate intent into action. As complexity increases, they spend more time interpreting priorities, resolving conflicts, and navigating ambiguity. Their effectiveness depends less on leadership clarity and more on their ability to manage congestion.

From their vantage point, the issue is not motivation or culture. It is flow.

This is the critical inflection point.

If leaders continue to rely on behaviour to carry exponential load, they become part of the constraint. Their presence, judgement, and reinforcement become necessary for progress. The organisation adapts around them rather than redesigning itself.

Alternatively, leaders can recognise that behaviour has reached its limit as a scaling mechanism.

This recognition does not diminish leadership. It repositions it.

Leadership shifts from modelling behaviour to designing capacity. From reinforcing culture to clarifying decision architecture. From setting standards to ensuring the system can meet them without heroic effort.

This shift is difficult because it requires leaders to stop doing what made them successful.

Behavioural excellence is deeply ingrained. It is rewarded. It is praised. It feels virtuous. Letting go of it as the primary lever feels risky.

Yet without this shift, excellence becomes a liability.

The organisation continues to demand high standards, but lacks the structure to sustain them efficiently. People compensate. Leaders intervene. Complexity grows. The gap widens.

This is not a temporary phase. It is a structural boundary.

Beyond a certain scale, greatness is no longer produced by behaviour alone. It requires design.

This chapter marks that boundary.

Why Many "Great" Companies Quietly Disappeared

Most great companies do not fail.

They erode.

This distinction matters, because erosion does not trigger alarm. It does not arrive with a crisis narrative or a single catastrophic decision. It unfolds gradually, beneath continued performance, until the organisation is no longer relevant enough to defend.

From the outside, this looks puzzling. Well led organisations with strong brands, capable people, and healthy finances slowly lose momentum. They are not overtaken overnight. They are simply outpaced.

The explanation is not incompetence. It is timing.

Market speed has changed faster than internal redesign cycles.

In earlier decades, organisations could rely on periodic transformation. A restructuring every few years. A strategy refresh. A new operating model. These interventions were disruptive, but infrequent. The environment allowed time for recovery and consolidation.

That rhythm no longer holds.

Markets now evolve continuously. Customer expectations shift faster. Technology compresses response windows. Competitive moves propagate quickly. The organisation does not face occasional shocks, but sustained pressure.

In this environment, redesign cannot be episodic. It must be structural and ongoing.

Many great companies continued to operate as though time was still available. Their internal redesign cadence lagged behind external change. By the time structural issues were acknowledged, the gap was already significant.

This is where erosion begins.

Success plays a central role in delaying reinvention.

When performance remains strong, the organisation has little incentive to question its foundations. Revenue validates existing models. Market position reinforces confidence. The leadership team focuses on execution, not redesign.

Reinvention feels unnecessary, even irresponsible, when results are positive.

What is missed is that the conditions producing those results are shifting. The organisation is solving yesterday's problems efficiently while tomorrow's pressures accumulate unnoticed.

This delay is not strategic blindness. It is rational behaviour in a context that has changed faster than the organisation's assumptions.

Operational drag increases silently during this period.

Processes accrete. Decision paths lengthen. Coordination overhead grows. Informal dependencies harden. None of this causes immediate failure. It simply slows response.

The organisation becomes less elastic.

When new opportunities appear, they take longer to evaluate. When threats emerge, they take longer to address. The cost of action rises. The cost of inaction remains hidden.

This asymmetry is dangerous.

Externally, competitors with lighter architectures move faster. They experiment cheaply. They adapt quickly. They are not necessarily better led. They are simply less burdened.

Internally, leaders sense the drag but struggle to locate its source. Performance metrics still look acceptable. Customer loss is incremental. Market share erodes slowly. The signals are noisy.

Because erosion is gradual, it is often attributed to external factors. Market maturity. Increased competition. Regulatory change. These explanations are not wrong, but they are incomplete.

What is rarely examined is whether the organisation's internal architecture is still matched to the speed and complexity of its environment.

Many great companies attempted to respond by adding capability rather than redesigning structure.

They invested in new technologies. They hired transformation leaders. They launched innovation initiatives. These actions created activity, but they did not address underlying drag. New capabilities were layered onto old architectures. Complexity increased further.

The organisation became busier, not faster.

This pattern repeats across industries and geographies.

Strong execution masks slow response. Capable people compensate for weak flow. Leaders intervene to maintain momentum. The organisation continues to operate, but its ability to adapt declines.

Over time, the gap between external speed and internal response becomes visible to the market.

Customers notice slower innovation. Partners sense hesitation. Talent becomes harder to retain. None of these signals are fatal on their own. Together, they indicate erosion.

The organisation is no longer failing. It is fading.

This is why many once great companies did not collapse. They merged. They were acquired. They restructured repeatedly. They survived, but they stopped shaping their markets.

From the inside, this transition often feels confusing. Leaders remember being decisive. They remember moving faster. They remember when success felt lighter.

The difference is not will or intelligence. It is architecture.

The organisation grew into a form that could no longer respond at the speed required. Its internal redesign lagged behind external change. Success delayed the moment of reckoning. Operational drag accumulated silently.

By the time the need for deep redesign was acknowledged, options were constrained. Changes became more disruptive. Costs increased. Cultural resistance hardened.

This is why erosion is more dangerous than failure.

Failure forces change. Erosion invites explanation.

Organisations rationalise decline because it is not yet dramatic. They adjust targets. They revise forecasts. They optimise margins. They manage the descent rather than arrest it.

The lesson here is not that greatness is fleeting by nature. It is that greatness is conditional.

It depends on an organisation's ability to redesign itself at least as fast as its environment changes. When that ability lags, erosion begins, regardless of past success.

This pattern is not obvious from inside the system. It is only visible when viewed structurally.

Great companies quietly disappeared not because they lost discipline or focus, but because the environment accelerated beyond what their architectures could carry. Their success delayed the recognition of that gap. Their competence prolonged the erosion.

Understanding this pattern is essential, because it removes false comfort.

If greatness can erode quietly, then performance alone is not proof of health. Stability is not assurance. Past success is not protection.

What matters is whether the organisation's structure is evolving in step with the world it operates in.

When it is not, disappearance does not arrive as a shock.

It arrives as a slow, almost polite, retreat from relevance.

The False Comfort of Legacy Playbooks

Legacy playbooks rarely fail outright. They comfort.

They are built from experience, validated by results, and reinforced by time. They carry the weight of past success, which gives them authority long after the conditions that produced that success have changed. This is why they are difficult to release. Not because they are wrong, but because they once worked.

Past frameworks become emotional anchors.

They stabilise decision making in uncertainty. They provide language, structure, and familiarity. Leaders return to them when pressure rises because they reduce ambiguity. In moments of complexity, familiarity feels like clarity.

The problem is not that leaders use these playbooks. It is that they stop questioning their fit.

What worked becomes unquestionable not through arrogance, but through reinforcement. The organisation has evidence. Results arrived. Markets responded. Careers advanced. The framework becomes part of identity. Challenging it feels like challenging the judgement that built the organisation in the first place.

This creates a subtle rigidity.

Leaders do not consciously resist change. They interpret new conditions through old lenses. Signals that do not fit the framework are discounted or reframed. The playbook becomes the filter through which reality is understood.

This is where precedent quietly overtakes observation.

Leaders over trust what has worked before because it reduces cognitive load. It shortens decision cycles. It provides a sense of control. In environments where change was incremental, this was an advantage. Precedent saved time and reduced risk.

In accelerated environments, precedent can obscure emerging constraints.

The organisation continues to apply familiar tools to unfamiliar problems. Strategy sessions repeat known formats. Transformation initiatives reuse established models. Metrics remain consistent even as relevance shifts. The organisation feels busy, but misaligned.

This is not complacency. It is continuity bias.

Familiar tools feel safer than redesign because redesign introduces uncertainty. It requires questioning assumptions, redistributing authority, and exposing hidden dependencies. It risks destabilising systems that are still producing results. In contrast, legacy playbooks promise improvement without disruption.

They offer optimisation instead of interrogation.

This is why many organisations respond to mounting complexity by refining existing processes rather than rethinking them. They add layers of governance. They increase reporting. They create new roles to manage interfaces. Each addition feels reasonable. Collectively, they increase drag.

The playbook expands, but the architecture remains unchanged.

At this stage, leaders often believe they are solving the problem. They are investing time, attention, and resources. They are not ignoring reality. They are engaging with it using tools that no longer map to its structure.

This is where internal confidence persists longest.

The organisation has answers. It has frameworks. It has experience. There is always another lever to pull, another initiative to launch, another refinement to attempt. The belief that the solution exists inside the system remains intact.

What changes quietly is effectiveness.

Each iteration produces less leverage. Improvements are marginal. Gains are local. Side effects increase. The organisation expends more effort to achieve smaller outcomes. The playbook still functions, but it no longer scales.

This is the false comfort.

Legacy frameworks provide reassurance that the situation is manageable through known means. They allow leaders to remain inside familiar territory. They delay the recognition that the problem is not one of execution, but of design.

This delay is costly, but not immediately visible.

While the organisation optimises within its existing architecture, the environment continues to move. Competitors redesign more radically. New entrants build without historical load. The gap widens, not because others are smarter, but because they are less constrained by precedent.

Eventually, leaders begin to feel a different kind of discomfort.

The playbook still offers answers, but those answers no longer feel proportionate to the challenge. Initiatives complete without producing momentum. Changes land without relieving pressure. The organisation does more, but feels no lighter.

This is often the point where leaders increase effort rather than question structure. They work harder to make the familiar work. They double down on execution. They protect the playbook because abandoning it feels like admitting failure.

What is actually required is not abandonment, but transcendence.

Legacy playbooks are not wrong. They are incomplete. They describe how to perform within a given architecture. They do not describe how to redesign that architecture when conditions change.

This is where readers stop trying to solve it alone.

Not because they lack intelligence or experience, but because they recognise a boundary. The tools that built the organisation cannot see the organisation clearly anymore. The system cannot diagnose itself without reinforcing its own assumptions.

This recognition is unsettling.

It challenges identity. It questions judgement. It introduces the possibility that success has created blind spots that competence alone cannot resolve. Leaders may resist this idea initially. That resistance is understandable.

Over time, it becomes difficult to ignore.

The organisation continues to demand more coordination, more oversight, more intervention. The playbook requires constant adaptation. Leaders feel responsible for making it work, even as it strains under the load.

At this point, the false comfort fades.

What remains is a quieter realisation. The problem is not execution. It is not discipline. It is not commitment. It is not a lack of frameworks.

It is that the architecture itself has outgrown the tools being used to manage it.

Legacy playbooks kept the organisation successful longer than it should have been. They extended performance. They delayed failure. They also postponed redesign.

Letting go of them does not mean rejecting the past. It means recognising that past success cannot design future capacity.

This is the moment where internal optimisation gives way to external perspective. Not as a preference, but as a necessity.

Because when the playbook becomes the constraint, the system cannot see beyond it.

PART III — From Leadership to Architecture, what carries weight

CHAPTER 3:
Invisible Load And Organisational Blindness

Why Proximity Destroys Visibility

Organisations do not become blind because leaders stop paying attention. They become blind because attention is placed too close to the work.

As seniority increases, proximity to execution increases. Leaders sit closer to decisions, escalations, exceptions, and issues. They are pulled into the flow of activity because that is where pressure surfaces. This feels necessary. It often is.

What changes quietly is visibility.

Seniority narrows signal.

At lower levels of the organisation, information is noisy but rich. Patterns emerge slowly, but variation is visible. People experience friction repeatedly and in context. They see where work stalls, where decisions loop, where effort is wasted. They may lack authority, but they have texture.

As leaders move upward, information becomes cleaner but thinner. Data is aggregated. Exceptions are summarised. Narratives replace experience. What reaches the top is filtered, shaped, and compressed. This is not manipulation. It is efficiency.

The cost of efficiency is loss of resolution.

Senior leaders see outcomes more clearly than process. They see results more readily than flow. They are exposed to what matters most urgently, not what matters most structurally. Over time, this changes how the organisation is perceived.

Involvement intensifies this effect.

When leaders are directly involved in solving problems, they influence the signal they are receiving. Their presence alters behaviour. Issues are framed differently. Work is prepared more carefully. Problems are escalated earlier or resolved quietly to avoid exposure.

This is not concealment. It is adaptation.

People respond to power. They simplify complexity when speaking upward. They focus on solvable elements. They avoid burdening senior leaders with ambiguity that feels unresolved. The system learns what to show.

As a result, leaders experience the organisation as more coherent than it actually is.

Diagnosis becomes distorted by participation.

When leaders are part of the solution path, they lose the ability to observe the system neutrally. They feel the pressure personally. They respond instinctively. They intervene to restore momentum. Each intervention changes the system's behaviour.

This makes cause and effect harder to see.

Leaders often believe they have exceptional visibility because they are involved everywhere. In reality, involvement reduces contrast. It becomes difficult to distinguish between what the system is doing on its own and what is happening because of leadership presence.

The organisation performs when the leader is there. The question of whether it performs without them becomes harder to answer.

Accountability further reduces perspective bandwidth.

As responsibility increases, leaders are held accountable for outcomes they do not fully control. This accountability focuses attention on delivery rather than diagnosis. Leaders become outcome oriented by necessity. They prioritise resolution over understanding.

This is rational. It is also limiting.

When leaders are accountable for results, they optimise for short-term stability. They fix issues quickly. They remove obstacles personally. They absorb risk. These actions protect performance, but they also suppress structural signals.

The organisation does not experience the consequence of poor design because leaders intercept it.

Over time, this creates a feedback loop.

The more leaders intervene, the less visible the underlying architecture becomes. The less visible it becomes, the more leaders must intervene to maintain performance. The system appears to function, but only under supervision.

This is organisational blindness created by proximity, not neglect.

A brief analogy clarifies this without overreach.

Standing inside a machine allows you to feel vibration, heat, and noise. You can tell something is wrong. You cannot see the machine's full structure while standing within it. To understand load paths and failure points, you must step back.

Leaders are standing inside their organisations.

Their closeness gives them immediacy, but it costs perspective. They feel pressure, but they cannot always see its source. They sense strain, but they attribute it to workload, people, or pace rather than design.

This blindness is reinforced by success.

When outcomes are achieved, the lack of visibility is not questioned. Performance validates perception. The organisation appears healthy because it is functioning. The effort required to sustain that function is normalised.

From the inside, the system feels demanding but manageable.

From a structural view, it is overloaded.

This is why many leaders struggle to articulate what feels wrong. They know something has shifted. They feel heavier. Decisions require more involvement. Coordination consumes more time. Yet there is no single failure to point to.

The blindness is not intellectual. It is positional.

Leaders cannot see the system clearly because they are part of its operating mechanism. Their actions are embedded in its flow. Their judgement compensates for its weaknesses. The organisation adapts around them.

Middle management experiences the opposite problem.

They see fragmentation and friction clearly, but lack authority to redesign. They feel the weight without the leverage to remove it. Their perspective is wide but constrained.

Between these two positions, structural reality is lost.

Senior leaders see outcomes without texture. Middle managers see texture without authority. No one sees the full load path.

This is why internal analysis so often circles familiar explanations. Productivity. Capability. Alignment. Culture. These are accessible lenses from within the system. Architecture is not.

To see architecture, leaders must regain distance from execution without abdicating responsibility. This is difficult, because stepping back feels like disengagement. It is not.

It is repositioning.

Until that repositioning occurs, leaders will continue to diagnose the organisation through the distortions created by proximity. They will see symptoms but not structure. They will fix issues but not causes.

This is not a failure of intelligence or intent. It is an inevitable consequence of how organisations scale and how leadership roles evolve.

Invisible load remains invisible not because it is hidden, but because the people best placed to redesign it are standing too close to see it.

This blindness is the precondition for everything that follows.

Decision Congestion, Not Strategy, Slows Growth

When growth slows, strategy is usually blamed first.

The organisation assumes the direction is wrong, the positioning is unclear, or the market has shifted. Leadership teams revisit vision. Consultants are asked to refine strategy decks. New initiatives are launched to re energise momentum.

In many cases, none of this addresses the real constraint.

Growth is rarely slowed by lack of strategic intent. It is slowed by the inability of the organisation to decide and act at the rate the strategy requires.

Decision congestion, not strategy, is the limiting factor.

In organisations under load, decisions begin to pile at the top. Not because leaders want control, but because the system routes uncertainty upward. Authority is unclear at the edges. Escalation becomes the safest path. Over time, senior leaders become the convergence point for choices that should not require their involvement.

Each escalation feels reasonable. Collectively, they create a bottleneck.

Leaders experience this as constant interruption. Calendars fill with approvals, clarifications, and sign offs. Decisions vary in importance, but all demand attention. Strategic time is fragmented by operational necessity.

From the outside, this looks like engaged leadership. From a structural perspective, it is congestion.

Authority is often the root cause.

As organisations grow, roles expand faster than decision rights are defined. Responsibilities are broad, but authority is conditional. Managers are accountable for outcomes without full permission to decide. When consequences feel asymmetric, people escalate.

This is rational behaviour.

Escalation replaces ownership because ownership without authority is risky. Teams seek validation not because they lack confidence, but because the system does not clearly support independent action. The organisation trains people to defer upward.

Over time, this pattern hardens.

Decisions that were once distributed become centralised. Leaders become involved earlier. The organisation moves slower even as it appears more controlled. Strategy remains clear, but execution falters.

Strategic intent is strangled not by disagreement, but by delay.

Plans exist. Priorities are articulated. The issue is translation. Each layer interprets intent cautiously. Hand offs multiply. Dependencies stack. By the time decisions are made, context has shifted.

The organisation is not failing to choose. It is choosing too slowly.

This congestion is rarely visible in strategy discussions. Strategy assumes a functioning execution system. It presumes that decisions will flow to where they are needed. When that flow breaks down, strategy becomes aspirational rather than operational.

Middle management feels this most acutely.

They are tasked with delivering outcomes while navigating unclear authority. They manage up to secure approvals and manage down to maintain momentum. Their effectiveness depends less on strategic clarity and more on their ability to unblock decisions.

They do not experience the problem as strategic confusion. They experience it as friction.

Projects stall waiting for sign off. Teams hesitate at boundaries. Meetings are scheduled to gain alignment that should already exist. Work slows at decision points, not because people disagree, but because no one is certain who should decide.

This is the signature of decision congestion.

Leaders often respond by adding structure in the wrong place.

More governance. More review forums. More escalation paths. These interventions increase visibility, but they also increase load. Decisions take longer. Bottlenecks intensify. The organisation becomes more cautious.

What is missing is decision architecture.

Decision architecture defines where decisions should sit, how they should move, and what authority accompanies responsibility. Without it, organisations rely on judgement and escalation. Under scale, this fails.

Strategy without flow is inert.

Even the most compelling strategic direction cannot overcome an organisation that cannot decide quickly and confidently. Growth stalls not because the destination is unclear, but because the path is blocked by indecision.

This is why organisations with similar strategies perform differently. The difference is not intent. It is throughput.

One organisation moves because decisions are resolved close to the work. Another stalls because decisions accumulate at the top. Both may articulate the same strategy. Only one can execute it at speed.

Decision congestion also distorts leadership perception.

Leaders believe they are heavily involved because the situation demands it. In reality, their involvement is demanded because the system lacks clarity. The more they intervene, the less pressure the system feels to resolve its own ambiguity.

This creates dependency.

The organisation learns that progress requires senior attention. Initiative narrows. Risk is deferred. Leaders become the gatekeepers of momentum.

From the outside, this looks like leadership strength. From a structural view, it is a design flaw.

Growth slows because the organisation cannot process decisions at the rate required by its environment. Strategy is constrained by capacity.

The uncomfortable truth is that many organisations do not need a new strategy. They need to redesign how decisions move.

Until decision congestion is addressed, strategic work becomes repetitive. Leaders revisit direction not because it is wrong, but because it is not translating into action. The organisation appears stuck in planning mode while execution lags.

This is not a failure of ambition or intelligence. It is a predictable outcome of growth without decision architecture.

Middle managers recognise this instinctively. They know the strategy. They believe in it. Their frustration lies in the mechanics of execution. They champion clarity not in vision, but in authority.

This chapter matters because it reframes the problem.

If growth is constrained by decision congestion, then solving it requires redesign, not inspiration. It requires shifting focus from what the organisation intends to do, to how it enables decisions to happen without friction.

Until that shift occurs, strategy will continue to feel sound while growth remains slow.

The bottleneck is not the plan. It is the flow.

Why Internal Fixes Eventually Fail

When pressure rises, organisations turn inward.

They assemble task forces. They commission internal reviews. They ask capable teams to diagnose what is slowing them down and to recommend improvements. This response feels responsible. It draws on institutional knowledge. It reinforces ownership.

For a time, it works.

Internal fixes deliver incremental relief. Processes are refined. Roles are clarified. Reporting improves. Bottlenecks ease temporarily. The organisation demonstrates responsiveness.

What is rarely questioned is whether internal fixes can ever address structural limitations.

Teams inside the organisation are optimised for delivery, not diagnosis.

They are rewarded for execution, continuity, and reliability. Their expertise is shaped by operating within the existing system. They understand how work gets done, where the shortcuts are, and which compromises are acceptable. This makes them effective operators.

It also constrains their diagnostic range.

Internal teams see problems through the lens of the structure they inhabit. They interpret friction as something to be managed, not redesigned. Their solutions fit the current architecture because that is what they know how to work with.

This is not a lack of intelligence. It is alignment with role.

Loyalty reinforces this constraint.

People who have grown with the organisation feel responsibility for its success. They defend what has worked. They protect colleagues and leaders. They avoid conclusions that imply foundational change because those conclusions feel disloyal.

This loyalty is a strength operationally. It is a weakness diagnostically.

It narrows the range of acceptable explanations. Structural issues are reframed as execution gaps. Design flaws are softened into training needs. Ambiguity is addressed with communication rather than clarity.

Internal reviews recycle assumptions.

They ask the right questions, but from within the same frame. They use familiar language. They reference existing frameworks. They validate past decisions. The outcome is usually a refined version of what already exists.

Change is incremental because it must be palatable. Radical redesign feels disproportionate when viewed from inside a system that is still functioning.

This creates a ceiling.

Internal fixes can optimise performance within current design limits. They cannot redefine those limits. The organisation improves at the margins while the core constraint remains intact.

Over time, this pattern becomes visible.

Each intervention produces less relief. Improvements are harder to sustain. New initiatives create side effects. Complexity increases. The organisation expends more effort coordinating fixes than benefiting from them.

At this stage, leaders often question execution rather than approach.

Why are the fixes not sticking?

Why does the same issue keep resurfacing?

Why does progress feel temporary?

The answer is not incompetence.

This is not incompetence. It is structural limitation.

Internal teams cannot see beyond the system they are part of. They cannot question assumptions that define their roles. They cannot redesign authority structures they depend on. They cannot remove load from leaders without redefining leadership itself.

These are not failures of will. They are boundaries of position.

The organisation asks itself to diagnose itself while preserving itself. That is an impossible task beyond a certain level of complexity.

This is why internal fixes eventually fail.

They are constrained by proximity, loyalty, and role design. They are effective at smoothing friction, but ineffective at revealing architecture. They address symptoms without disturbing the structure that produces them.

The organisation experiences a cycle of hope and frustration.

Each new initiative promises relief. Each delivers some improvement. Each fails to produce lasting lightness. Over time, cynicism grows. Change fatigue sets in. Leaders become wary of new efforts because previous ones did not hold.

This fatigue is often misinterpreted as resistance to change.

In reality, it is evidence that the system has reached its internal limits.

There is a point where further optimisation becomes counterproductive. Where adding more process, more governance, or more initiatives increases load rather than reducing it. Internal fixes reach diminishing returns.

At that point, the organisation faces a choice it rarely articulates.

Continue optimising within known boundaries, accepting slower growth and increased effort, or confront the possibility that the structure itself must be redesigned.

That confrontation is difficult from inside.

It challenges identity. It questions past decisions. It requires removing dependencies that feel essential. It disrupts relationships that have formed around the existing system.

This is why internal resolution feels preferable, even when it no longer works.

The illusion persists because the organisation has not yet failed. Performance still holds. The pain is manageable. There is always another adjustment to try.

Eventually, the illusion breaks.

Either external pressure forces change, or leaders recognise that the system cannot see itself clearly enough to redesign itself. This recognition is not defeat. It is realism.

Internal fixes fail not because people are incapable, but because architecture cannot be redesigned from within its own constraints.

This is the final illusion that must fall before meaningful change becomes possible.

Until it does, the organisation will continue to work hard at solving problems it is not structurally equipped to resolve.

And effort, at this stage, only deepens the limitation.

The Cost of Waiting Until Pain Is Obvious

Most organisations do not change when clarity is available. They change when pain removes alternatives.

This is not a failure of leadership. It is a predictable response to uncertainty. As long as performance holds and pressure feels manageable, delay appears rational. Leaders prioritise stability. They avoid disruption. They protect momentum.

What is underestimated is the cost of waiting.

Optionality shrinks under pressure.

In early stages of strain, organisations still have room to manoeuvre. Redesign can be selective. Authority can be clarified gradually. Systems can be adjusted without destabilising operations. People are receptive because change feels proactive rather than reactive.

As pressure increases, options narrow.

Dependencies harden. Informal workarounds become formalised. Leaders become indispensable. Talent adapts to the system rather than questioning it. The organisation loses flexibility without noticing.

By the time pain is obvious, the architecture is already fixed around compensations.

Late intervention costs more because it must unwind habits that have become essential. Decisions that should have been redistributed now require deliberate extraction from leadership. Processes that evolved organically must be rebuilt under live conditions. Relationships formed around ambiguity must be redefined.

This is disruptive, not because change is happening, but because it is happening too late.

The organisation experiences redesign as shock rather than evolution.

Costs increase accordingly.

Change requires more communication. Resistance is stronger. Productivity dips. Leaders must manage transition while still delivering results. What could have been a targeted adjustment becomes a broad intervention.

None of this is visible when delay feels comfortable.

This is why leaders act when pain forces clarity, not when clarity is available.

Clarity alone rarely justifies disruption. It feels theoretical. Pain provides justification. It removes doubt. It aligns stakeholders because the alternative is worse.

The danger is that pain arrives after optionality has already been lost.

When markets tighten, when margins compress, when talent leaves, or when customers shift, the organisation must change under pressure. Decisions are rushed. Trade offs are harsher. The organisation accepts solutions it would have rejected earlier

What might have been designed becomes imposed.

This is the hidden cost of waiting.

Early signals offered clarity without urgency. They were explainable. Manageable. Easy to defer. Leaders chose stability, believing they could act later if needed.

Later arrives with constraints.

The organisation no longer has the freedom to choose timing, sequencing, or scope. Change happens in response to events rather than by design. Leaders lose the ability to protect core strengths while redesigning weaknesses.

Optionality has collapsed.

This is not dramatic. It is incremental.

Each month of delay slightly reduces flexibility. Each workaround makes redesign harder. Each dependency increases the cost of removal. None of these changes feel decisive at the time.

The organisation still functions. Performance still holds. The sense of urgency remains low.

This is why waiting is so common.

Leaders are rational actors. They balance risk and reward. They avoid unnecessary disruption. They respond to evidence.

What they often underestimate is how quickly structural debt compounds.

Unlike financial debt, structural debt does not demand immediate repayment. It accrues quietly. Interest is paid in effort, coordination, and leadership bandwidth. As long as that payment is affordable, the debt feels manageable.

Eventually, the payment exceeds capacity.

At that point, leaders are forced to act, but from a weaker position. The organisation has fewer options. The margin for error is smaller. The tolerance for disruption is lower.

Urgency replaces intention.

This chapter is not an argument for panic. It is an argument for timing.

Change undertaken early is calmer, cheaper, and more precise. Change undertaken late is reactive, expensive, and disruptive. The difference is not insight. It is choice.

Most leaders do not wait because they are unaware. They wait because the system still appears to function. The pain is distributed. The cost is invisible. The organisation adapts.

By the time pain concentrates, the opportunity to redesign gracefully has passed.

This is the inevitability leaders eventually confront.

They can either act when clarity is available, preserving optionality, or act when pain demands it, accepting constraint. The system does not offer a third option.

Waiting does not maintain the status quo. It quietly narrows the future.

When pain becomes obvious, it is not a signal to begin thinking. It is a signal that thinking has been deferred too long.

At that point, the organisation no longer asks whether change is needed.

It asks how much it can afford to lose while making it.

That question arrives late.

And by then, the cost has already been set.

PART IV — The Five Pillars, making greatness load-bearing

CHAPTER 4:
When Structure, Not Effort, Becomes The Difference

The Shift from Performance to Capacity

For a long time, greatness was measured by performance.

Revenue growth. Market share. Margins. Execution against plan. These indicators made sense in an environment where pressure was episodic and time allowed correction. Performance signalled competence. Sustained performance suggested excellence.

What has changed is not the value of performance, but its meaning.

Performance describes what an organisation produces under current conditions. Capacity describes what it can absorb when conditions change. The two are no longer interchangeable.

In modern organisations, performance can remain high even as capacity erodes. Results can be delivered through effort, coordination, and leadership intervention long after the underlying structure has reached its limits. This creates a dangerous illusion. The organisation appears strong while becoming increasingly fragile.

Capacity absorbs pressure. Performance consumes it.

An organisation with capacity responds to volatility without distortion. Decisions move without congestion. Teams adapt without escalation. Leaders retain altitude. Pressure reveals issues early, not catastrophically. The system flexes because it was designed to.

An organisation driven by performance behaves differently. It meets targets by increasing effort. It absorbs shocks through heroics. It relies on leadership bandwidth to compensate for weak flow. Pressure is managed, not absorbed. Over time, this management becomes exhausting.

Performance burns people when it substitutes for design.

This burn is not always visible as disengagement or turnover. Often, it shows up as narrowing. Leaders focus on what they can control. Teams avoid risk. Initiative contracts. The organisation becomes conservative not by intention, but by fatigue.

Excellence under these conditions is expensive.

Each unit of output costs more attention. Each improvement requires more coordination. The organisation still performs, but it does so by consuming its own capacity. Leaders spend the organisation's future to protect its present.

Design outlasts effort because it does not rely on will.

Effort is finite. Attention degrades under load. Judgement suffers when stretched. No leader, however capable, can remain the load bearing element of a complex system indefinitely. Design, by contrast, persists. It carries weight repeatedly without exhaustion.

This is the pivot point for modern greatness.

Greatness is no longer defined by how well an organisation performs when everything is aligned. It is defined by how little effort is required to perform when conditions are not. It is revealed under pressure, not during stability.

This reframing unsettles many leaders because it challenges long held instincts. Performance has been rewarded for decades. Careers have been built on it. Organisations have been structured to maximise it. Shifting attention away from performance feels counterintuitive.

The shift is not away from results. It is away from how results are produced.

Capacity is upstream of performance. It determines whether performance is sustainable, transferable, and resilient. Without capacity, performance becomes brittle. It depends on specific people, specific conditions, and constant intervention.

This brittleness is often misinterpreted as ambition.

Leaders push harder. Teams stretch further. The organisation celebrates resilience. In reality, it is compensating. The cost is paid quietly in fatigue, congestion, and lost optionality.

A capacity led organisation behaves differently.

When pressure increases, it does not immediately escalate. Decisions resolve closer to the work. Authority is clear enough to act without permission seeking. Systems guide behaviour without constant reinforcement. Leaders observe more than they intervene.

This is not because people are less committed. It is because the structure is doing its job.

The distinction becomes visible during change.

When a performance driven organisation faces disruption, it reacts by mobilising effort. Task forces are formed. Leaders dive in. Communication intensifies. Progress is achieved, but at high cost. Once the crisis passes, the organisation is depleted.

When a capacity driven organisation faces the same disruption, response is uneven but contained. Some areas strain, others adapt. The system reveals its limits without collapsing. Redesign is informed by real signals rather than exhaustion.

The difference is not speed. It is sustainability.

This is why design outlasts effort.

Design determines how work flows when no one is watching. It defines how decisions are made under ambiguity. It establishes what happens when leaders are unavailable. These conditions expose whether greatness is real or performative.

The challenge for leaders is that capacity does not announce itself through metrics that boards traditionally celebrate. It is not immediately visible in quarterly results. It reveals itself in how little drama accompanies pressure.

This makes it easy to deprioritise.

Performance is rewarded publicly. Capacity is noticed only when absent.

By the time absence is visible, the organisation is already constrained. Redesign becomes urgent and disruptive. Leaders are forced to act from within the pressure they failed to design for.

The philosophical shift, grounded in structural reality, is this.

Greatness is not the ability to deliver exceptional outcomes repeatedly. It is the ability to do so without consuming the people responsible for delivery. It is not about how hard the organisation can push. It is about how much it can carry.

Capacity absorbs pressure so that effort can be reserved for progress, not survival.

This does not diminish ambition. It protects it.

Organisations built on capacity can pursue opportunity without fear of collapse. They can decentralise without losing coherence. They can scale without concentrating risk. They can survive leadership transition without loss of momentum.

These attributes are not cultural aspirations. They are design outcomes.

This is why structure, not effort, becomes the difference.

Effort will always matter. Commitment will always matter. Discipline will always matter. But none of these can compensate for architecture that cannot carry load. When they are asked to, they fail silently, by burning people rather than revealing limits.

The shift from performance to capacity is not optional in the current environment. It is imposed by speed, complexity, and volatility. Leaders can either recognise it early or experience it late.

This section marks the pivot away from trying harder and toward building something that holds.

From this point forward, greatness is no longer judged by how much the organisation can achieve.

It is judged by how little strain it requires to do so.

The Three Forces That Actually Carry Scale

Scale is often described as growth multiplied. In practice, it is pressure multiplied.

As organisations grow, they are subjected to forces that do not simply add complexity, they compound it. Direction must travel further. Decisions must move faster. Value must be created repeatedly without degrading quality. Movement must continue even when leaders are absent.

Most organisations attempt to manage this by increasing effort. Some refine strategy. Others invest in capability. Many focus on culture. These interventions help at the margins, but they do not address what actually carries scale.

Scale is not carried by enthusiasm, intent, or aspiration. It is carried by a small set of structural forces working together. When they are aligned, the organisation moves with surprising ease. When they are not, effort explodes.

The first force is direction.

Direction is not vision in the inspirational sense. It is coherence. It is the ability of the organisation to answer, consistently and unambiguously, what matters now, what matters next, and what does not matter at all.

Direction without cadence fails.

In many organisations, direction exists as a statement rather than a mechanism. Leaders articulate priorities clearly, sometimes repeatedly. Teams understand the intent. The problem is not confusion. It is decay.

Without cadence, direction dissipates as it moves through the organisation. Each layer interprets it slightly differently. Trade offs are made locally. Urgency varies. Over time, alignment frays.

The organisation does not drift because people ignore direction. It drifts because direction is not reinforced structurally. It is not embedded into how decisions are reviewed, how priorities are sequenced, or how progress is assessed.

Direction that relies on memory, communication, or leadership presence is fragile. It holds only while attention is sustained. Under pressure, it collapses into competing interpretations.

Scale requires direction that is renewed rhythmically, not restated occasionally. Without that rhythm, even the clearest intent loses force.

The second force is value.

Value is often discussed in terms of proposition or differentiation. Structurally, value is flow. It is the organisation's ability to convert effort into outcomes reliably, repeatedly, and at increasing volume.

Value without flow drifts.

When flow is weak, value creation becomes inconsistent. Bottlenecks emerge. Work queues. Hand offs multiply. The organisation produces outcomes, but not predictably. Quality varies. Delivery depends on who is involved rather than on how the system operates.

In this state, value feels present but unstable.

Leaders often respond by tightening controls or increasing oversight. These actions protect output in the short term, but they further restrict flow. The organisation becomes careful rather than capable.

True value at scale depends on flow that does not require constant supervision. Decisions move to where information lives. Work progresses without escalation. Exceptions are rare enough to be meaningful.

Without this, value creation drifts away from intent. The organisation works hard, but the connection between effort and outcome weakens. Teams lose sight of how their work contributes. Leaders lose confidence in forecasts.

Value without flow is effort intensive. It consumes attention rather than generating leverage.

The third force is movement.

Movement is not activity. It is momentum. It is the organisation's ability to progress initiatives without stalling, looping, or reverting under pressure.

Movement without structure collapses.

In many organisations, movement depends on energy. Leaders push. Teams respond. Progress is achieved through urgency. This works until it does not.

As complexity increases, energy based movement becomes erratic. Some initiatives surge while others stall. Priorities compete. Progress depends on intervention. The organisation moves, but not coherently.

Structure stabilises movement.

Structure defines how initiatives start, how they are reviewed, how conflicts are resolved, and how resources are reallocated. Without it, movement is vulnerable to disruption. Every change in priority creates turbulence. Every new initiative competes for attention.

This is why scale often feels like chaos rather than growth.

When direction, value, and movement are misaligned, the organisation compensates with effort. Leaders intervene. Meetings increase. Coordination intensifies. Progress continues, but at escalating cost.

When these forces align, something different happens.

Direction is clear and reinforced through rhythm. Value is created through flow rather than heroics. Movement is supported by structure rather than driven by pressure. The organisation feels lighter even as it grows.

This alignment is rarely named explicitly. It is experienced.

Leaders notice fewer escalations. Teams act with confidence. Decisions resolve faster. Progress feels steady rather than frantic. The organisation absorbs change without drama.

Importantly, this alignment does not eliminate difficulty. It changes where difficulty shows up. Problems surface earlier. Constraints become visible. Redesign is informed rather than reactive.

This is what actually carries scale.

Not ambition. Not talent. Not effort. Those are inputs. The carrying capacity of an organisation is determined by how these three forces interact under load.

Direction that is not renewed structurally becomes noise. Value that is not supported by flow becomes fragile. Movement that is not grounded in structure becomes chaos.

Most organisations have all three elements present in some form. Few have them aligned.

This misalignment explains why growth feels harder than expected. Why success requires more coordination than it should. Why leaders feel constantly involved. Why progress depends on intervention.

The organisation is attempting to scale on effort rather than on design.

This section matters because it reframes the problem without prescribing a solution. It introduces a lens through which leaders can interpret what they are already experiencing.

If direction requires constant reinforcement, cadence is missing. If value creation feels unstable, flow is compromised. If movement depends on pressure, structure is absent.

These are not cultural issues. They are architectural ones.

Later, these forces will be named and formalised. For now, they serve as a diagnostic bridge. They explain why scale feels heavier than it should and why effort alone cannot carry what the organisation is attempting to do.

Greatness at scale is not accidental. It is not inspirational. It is engineered.

These three forces are the load bearing elements.

When they are misaligned, no amount of leadership effort will compensate for long.

Why Systems, Staffing, and Decisions Must Be Designed Together

Organisations rarely fail because one element is missing. They fail because elements are designed in isolation.

Systems are improved without considering who must operate them. People are hired without redesigning how work flows. Decisions are decentralised without clarifying authority or support. Each change makes sense locally. Collectively, they create imbalance.

This imbalance is one of the most persistent sources of invisible load.

Systems without people fail.

Processes, tools, and platforms are often introduced to create efficiency, control, or consistency. On paper, they work. In practice, they depend on the people who must interpret, maintain, and use them. When systems are designed without regard for human capacity, they become brittle.

People work around them. Exceptions multiply. Manual intervention increases. The system exists, but flow does not improve. The organisation gains complexity without leverage.

This is not a technology problem. It is a design problem.

Systems assume certain behaviours, skills, and decision rights. When those assumptions are wrong, the system adds work rather than removing it. The organisation becomes dependent on individuals who know how to navigate the system rather than on the system itself.

Over time, this dependence concentrates knowledge and increases risk.

People without systems burn out.

At the other extreme, organisations rely on capability instead of structure. They hire strong performers, empower them broadly, and expect results. For a while, this works. Talented people adapt. They solve problems creatively. They bridge gaps.

As complexity increases, the cost of this adaptation rises.

Without systems to support them, people become the glue holding work together. They coordinate manually. They remember context. They compensate for missing clarity. Their effectiveness depends on constant effort.

Burnout is not the first symptom. Narrowing is.

People stop taking risks. They protect their bandwidth. They focus on immediate deliverables. Long term improvement is deferred because survival takes precedence. The organisation loses capacity even as headcount increases.

This is often misread as a talent issue.

Leaders conclude they need better people. They hire more experienced managers. They increase expectations. The underlying problem remains. The system is still absent.

Growth without transferability traps leaders.

Transferability is the organisation's ability to produce outcomes independent of specific individuals. It is the difference between a system that works because someone is present and one that works because it is designed to.

When systems, staffing, and decisions are not designed together, transferability collapses.

Leaders become essential nodes. Certain individuals become indispensable. Knowledge is tacit. Authority is informal. The organisation functions, but only under supervision.

This trap is subtle because it feels like strength.

Leaders are involved. Teams are responsive. Problems are solved quickly. Performance holds. From the outside, the organisation appears robust.

From the inside, it is fragile.

Any attempt to step back creates anxiety. Delegation feels risky. Succession becomes theoretical. Growth increases dependency rather than reducing it.

This is not because leaders refuse to let go. It is because the system cannot function without them.

The root cause is separation.

Systems are designed as if people were interchangeable. People are hired as if systems will adapt. Decisions are distributed without ensuring that authority, information, and capability align.

Each element is optimised independently. The organisation as a whole becomes inefficient.

Architectural integration resolves this.

When systems, staffing, and decisions are designed together, each reinforces the others.

Systems are built to support the way people actually work. They reduce cognitive load rather than increase it. They make the right actions easier and the wrong ones harder.

Staffing is aligned to roles with clear decision rights. People know what they own, what they can decide, and when to escalate. Capability is matched to responsibility.

Decisions flow through defined paths. Authority is explicit. Escalation is reserved for exceptions, not used as a default.

In this integrated state, effort produces leverage.

People spend less time compensating and more time creating. Systems carry routine load. Leaders focus on design rather than intervention. The organisation becomes lighter without becoming lax.

This integration is rarely achieved through incremental fixes.

Organisations often improve one element at a time. They upgrade systems. They restructure teams. They redefine decision rights. Each change improves a local condition, but may worsen another.

For example, introducing a new system without adjusting roles creates confusion. Decentralising decisions without support systems creates risk. Hiring senior people into poorly designed roles creates frustration.

The organisation experiences change fatigue because improvements conflict.

Integration requires stepping above individual initiatives and designing the organisation as a whole. This perspective is difficult to achieve from inside the system because each function optimises for its own outcomes.

The result is architectural debt.

As the organisation grows, the lack of integration becomes more costly. Coordination overhead increases. Leaders intervene more frequently. Transferability declines.

This is the moment where many organisations become stuck.

They know something is wrong. They have invested in people, systems, and processes. They have improved many parts. Yet the whole remains heavy.

The missing element is not effort or commitment. It is integration.

Designing systems, staffing, and decisions together is not an abstract ideal. It is a practical necessity for scale. Without it, growth amplifies friction. With it, growth creates leverage.

This section introduces a simple but often ignored truth.

No organisation can scale sustainably if its systems assume one reality, its people operate in another, and its decisions follow a third. Alignment is not cultural. It is structural.

When these elements are integrated, the organisation begins to carry its own weight.

When they are not, leaders will continue to do so.

And that is not greatness.

The Moment Leaders Stop Carrying the Organisation Personally

There is a moment leaders often describe only in hindsight.

The organisation still has problems. Pressure still exists. Complexity has not disappeared. Yet something fundamental has shifted. The weight no longer sits in the same place.

Leaders stop carrying the organisation personally.

This moment is not marked by an announcement or a change in title. It is felt as relief, but not relief from responsibility. Relief from distortion. The kind that comes when effort is no longer being used to compensate for design.

Leadership load begins to redistribute.

Decisions that once escalated automatically now resolve closer to the work. Not because leaders have withdrawn, but because authority has been clarified and supported. Teams act without waiting. Managers decide without rehearsing justification. Escalation becomes meaningful again because it is reserved for true exceptions.

This redistribution does not reduce leadership importance. It restores it.

Leaders move from being throughput to being architects of throughput. Their attention is no longer consumed by volume. It is freed for pattern recognition, sequencing, and anticipation. They regain the ability to see ahead rather than react.

Decisions move back into structure.

This shift is subtle but profound. Meetings change character. Conversations move from approval to insight. Updates become signals rather than requests. Leaders are informed rather than required.

The organisation does not move faster because people are pushing harder. It moves faster because fewer decisions are waiting for permission. Flow improves without drama. Progress feels steadier, less brittle.

Importantly, this does not feel like loss of control.

It feels like control returning to where it belongs.

Leaders often discover that much of what they were carrying did not require their judgement. It required clarity. Once clarity exists, the system absorbs load naturally. Leaders intervene less not because they are disengaged, but because intervention is no longer necessary.

This is the moment leaders regain altitude.

Altitude is not distance. It is perspective.

From altitude, patterns become visible. Interdependencies are clearer. Constraints reveal themselves earlier. Leaders can distinguish between noise and signal because they are no longer immersed in execution.

This perspective changes the quality of leadership.

Decisions are fewer but more consequential. Time is spent designing future capacity rather than managing present friction. Pressure is interpreted rather than absorbed. Leaders are no longer the first line of defence.

The organisation feels lighter not because work has decreased, but because weight is being carried by design.

Middle management experiences this shift as trust.

They no longer need to translate intent repeatedly. They are not required to manage up constantly. Their role shifts from coordination to delivery. Their judgement is exercised rather than deferred.

Teams experience it as confidence.

They know where decisions sit. They understand priorities. They act without hesitation. Mistakes surface earlier and are resolved faster. Learning replaces caution.

None of this requires motivation. It emerges from structure.

This is why the moment feels like release.

Leaders realise that much of their exhaustion was not caused by volume, but by misplacement of load. They were carrying decisions, context, and coordination that should have been embedded in the organisation.

Once redistributed, effort converts back into leverage.

The organisation still requires leadership. It still faces complexity. But leadership energy is now used to shape the system rather than prop it up. The difference is immediately felt.

Calendars open slightly. Conversations deepen. Strategic thinking returns. Leaders are present without being consumed.

This moment often arrives quietly.

There is no celebration. No declaration of success. Just an observable change in how the organisation behaves under pressure. Fewer escalations. Clearer ownership. Less urgency driven by anxiety.

The organisation has not become perfect. It has become capable.

This capability is what allows greatness to endure.

When leaders stop carrying the organisation personally, they do not become less responsible. They become more effective. They create conditions where the organisation can function without constant supervision.

This is the difference between leadership as effort and leadership as design.

The emotional release comes from recognising that the burden was never meant to be personal. It was structural. Once addressed structurally, the strain lifts naturally.

Leaders often describe this moment as regaining control. In reality, they are regaining perspective.

They are no longer inside the system absorbing shock. They are above it, shaping how shock is absorbed.

This is not abdication. It is maturity.

And it marks the point where greatness stops being dependent on individuals and starts being carried by the organisation itself.

From here, leadership becomes what it was always meant to be.

Not a load bearing function, but a design discipline.

PART V:
The Five Laws of Architectural Intelligence, how to see what you cannot see inside

CHAPTER 5

The Five Laws Leaders Must Obey

Law 1: Structure Reveals Truth Before People Do

Pressure does not create problems. It reveals them.

When conditions tighten, leaders often look to effort for explanation. People must be tired. Teams must be stretched. Standards must be slipping. These interpretations are intuitive because effort is visible and personal. Structure is neither.

Yet pressure does not test will. It tests design.

Effort can compensate for weak structure temporarily. Pressure removes that compensation. It strips away the margin that allowed individuals to bridge gaps quietly. What remains is the organisation as it actually is.

This is why pressure is diagnostic.

Under pressure, the organisation behaves more honestly. Decisions queue where authority is unclear. Work stalls where flow is broken. Escalations increase where design is incomplete. These responses are not failures of character. They are predictable reactions to load.

Pressure exposes design limits, not effort limits.

When leaders treat pressure as a crisis, they respond by increasing control. More oversight. Faster escalation. Tighter reporting. These actions can stabilise outcomes briefly, but they obscure the signal pressure is providing. The organisation adapts to intervention rather than revealing its constraints.

The opportunity is lost.

To read pressure correctly, leaders must resist the instinct to fix immediately. They must observe where pressure accumulates and why. Not who is struggling, but where the system is unable to carry load without distortion.

There are consistent patterns.

Pressure concentrates at decision boundaries. Where authority is ambiguous, decisions slow. Where accountability is shared, ownership dissolves. Where priorities conflict, escalation replaces resolution. These are not behavioural issues. They are structural signals.

Pressure also reveals false redundancy.

Processes that appeared robust under normal conditions collapse when volume increases. Informal workarounds fail. Knowledge held by individuals becomes a bottleneck. The organisation discovers which parts of its operation were never designed to scale.

None of this is visible during stability.

During stable periods, effort masks fragility. People adapt. Leaders intervene. Systems appear to function. Pressure removes the mask.

This is why leaders often feel blindsided by breakdowns that, in hindsight, were predictable. The signals were present, but muted. Pressure amplified them.

Reading pressure as a signal requires a different posture.

Instead of asking, "How do we get through this?" leaders ask, "What is this telling us about the system?" Instead of focusing on relief, they focus on revelation. Where is work accumulating? Where are decisions waiting? Where does progress depend on specific individuals?

These questions do not blame. They illuminate.

One of the most common misinterpretations of pressure is to treat it as evidence that the organisation is being asked to do too much. Sometimes that is true. More often, it is being asked to do things in a way the structure cannot support.

Volume alone is rarely the problem. Flow is.

An organisation with sufficient capacity can absorb significant pressure without panic. Decisions still move. Priorities remain clear. Leaders remain available for strategic work. The experience is demanding but contained.

An organisation with insufficient capacity reacts differently. Pressure creates noise. Urgency replaces clarity. Leaders are pulled into execution. The organisation survives, but at the cost of coherence.

The difference is not resilience. It is design.

Another error leaders make is to attribute pressure responses to culture.

They conclude that teams are risk averse, siloed, or resistant. In reality, teams are responding rationally to incentives and constraints. If escalation is the safest path, people escalate. If waiting avoids blame, people wait. Culture follows structure under pressure.

This is why structural signals are more reliable than behavioural interpretations.

Behaviour changes with mood, leadership presence, and context. Structure changes slowly. When pressure produces the same bottlenecks repeatedly, the issue is not attitude. It is architecture.

Leaders who learn to read pressure gain an advantage.

They stop chasing symptoms. They stop reorganising personalities. They stop treating exhaustion as the primary problem. Instead, they identify where the system cannot carry load without intervention.

This shifts intervention upstream.

Rather than asking people to cope better, leaders redesign decision paths. Rather than adding oversight, they clarify authority. Rather than increasing meetings, they remove dependencies.

Pressure becomes useful.

It highlights where the organisation must change to survive acceleration. It shows where effort is being misapplied. It reveals which parts of the organisation are brittle and which are resilient.

This does not mean leaders should seek pressure. It means they should not waste it.

Pressure is inevitable in modern environments. Volatility, speed, and complexity ensure it. The question is whether pressure is treated as a threat to be suppressed or as information to be interpreted.

Most organisations choose suppression.

They stabilise through heroics. They manage crises. They reward those who absorb shock. The organisation returns to baseline, but nothing fundamental changes. The same patterns reappear under the next wave of pressure.

This is how structural debt compounds.

Leaders who treat pressure as a signal do something different.

They allow the organisation to feel the strain long enough to see its source. They resist the urge to immediately intervene everywhere. They prioritise redesign over relief.

This requires discipline.

It also requires confidence. Leaders must tolerate short term discomfort to gain long term clarity. They must trust that revealing weakness is safer than hiding it.

The reward is precision.

Instead of broad transformation, leaders make targeted architectural changes. They remove specific bottlenecks. They redesign specific decision rights. They reinforce specific flows. The organisation becomes more capable without becoming heavier.

Pressure stops being something to fear. It becomes a test the organisation can learn from.

Law 1 establishes a foundational principle.

Before people feel overwhelmed, structure is already failing. Before results decline, capacity is already exceeded. Before leaders burn out, the system has already shifted load onto them.

Pressure reveals these truths early.

Leaders who can read pressure accurately do not wait for pain to force change. They recognise inevitability while optionality remains.

That ability marks the difference between organisations that erode quietly and those that redesign deliberately.

Structure speaks before people do.

Pressure is its language.

Law 2: Load Always Transfers, It Never Disappears

Organisations often believe they are removing load when they intervene. In reality, they are relocating it.

When a bottleneck appears, leaders act. They add resources. They escalate decisions. They insert oversight. They intervene personally.

The immediate problem eases. Progress resumes. From the inside, it feels like resolution.

Structurally, something else has happened.

The load has moved.

Load is not eliminated by effort. It is redistributed by design. When one part of the system cannot carry weight, that weight shifts to another part, often without being recognised. The organisation feels relief in one area while strain increases elsewhere.

This is why firefighting feels effective and costly at the same time.

Firefighting solves the visible problem by absorbing pressure locally. Leaders step in. Teams rally. Exceptions are handled. Delivery resumes. The organisation survives the moment.

The cost is hidden.

Each firefight teaches the system where to send load next time. Escalation becomes the path of least resistance. Certain teams become shock absorbers. Leaders become the default resolution mechanism. The organisation learns that structure is optional because effort will compensate.

Load does not disappear. It concentrates.

One of the most common examples is leadership intervention.

When leaders personally resolve issues, they remove pressure from teams temporarily. The decision is made. The conflict is resolved. Work moves forward. What is not addressed is why the decision had to escalate in the first place.

The load that should have been carried by clear authority, defined process, or designed flow is now carried by leadership bandwidth.

Over time, this bandwidth saturates.

Leaders feel busier. Calendars fill. Strategic time erodes. The organisation continues to function, but only because leaders are absorbing load that should not belong to them.

Another common transfer occurs between teams.

When one team struggles to deliver, another compensates. Deadlines are pulled forward. Dependencies are reworked informally. Work is rerouted. The system adapts.

This adaptation is rarely visible at the organisational level. Metrics still look acceptable. Customers are served. Targets are met.

The cost is fragmentation.

Teams operate outside defined boundaries. Accountability blurs. Coordination increases. Informal agreements replace formal design. The organisation becomes harder to manage because it no longer behaves predictably.

Load has moved from process into people.

Firefighting accelerates this transfer.

In moments of urgency, design is suspended. Rules are bypassed. Exceptions become normal. Leaders praise responsiveness. Teams are rewarded for flexibility.

These behaviours are rational under pressure. They are damaging when normalised.

Each exception weakens the system's ability to carry future load. Each workaround creates dependency. Each bypass trains the organisation to route pressure away from structure and toward effort.

This is how hidden debt accumulates.

Unlike financial debt, structural debt is not recorded. It does not appear on balance sheets. It is paid through coordination, fatigue, and loss of optionality. Interest is charged daily, but quietly.

Teams feel it as constant urgency. Leaders feel it as diminishing leverage. The organisation feels it as heaviness.

The most dangerous aspect of load transfer is that it creates the illusion of progress.

Problems are solved. Crises are averted. Performance holds. Leaders receive positive feedback for stepping in. Teams feel supported.

The organisation concludes that the approach works.

What it does not see is that each intervention makes the next one more likely.

As load transfers repeatedly, certain parts of the organisation become chronic carriers. Specific leaders. Specific teams. Specific roles. These areas become essential, not because they were designed to be, but because the system depends on them.

This dependency is fragile.

When carriers are absent, overloaded, or removed, the system struggles. What appeared resilient reveals itself as brittle. The organisation discovers that it was functioning through compensation, not capacity.

This discovery often arrives late.

Because load transfer preserves performance, it delays redesign. Leaders believe they are buying time. In reality, they are narrowing options. The longer load is carried informally, the harder it becomes to reassign it structurally.

Removing load from individuals requires redesigning authority, process, and flow. This is disruptive once dependencies have formed. The organisation resists because compensation has become normal.

This is why firefighting creates hidden debt across teams.

Each fire extinguished through effort adds weight somewhere else. The organisation becomes a network of compensations rather than a coherent system. Leaders lose sight of where load actually sits.

Eventually, the system reaches a point where there is nowhere left for load to go.

Leaders are saturated. Teams are stretched. Processes are bypassed. The organisation feels constantly urgent. At this stage, any additional pressure causes disproportionate disruption.

This is often misinterpreted as fragility in people.

In reality, it is fragility in design.

Understanding this law changes how leaders intervene.

Instead of asking how to remove pressure, they ask where pressure is moving. Instead of celebrating resolution, they examine redistribution. Instead of rewarding heroics, they question what made heroics necessary.

This perspective does not eliminate the need for intervention. It reframes it.

Sometimes leaders must absorb load to protect the organisation. The difference is whether that absorption is treated as a signal for redesign or as a sustainable solution.

If it is treated as a solution, debt accumulates. If it is treated as information, capacity increases.

Load always transfers. It never disappears.

Leaders who ignore this law create organisations that survive through constant compensation. Leaders who respect it design organisations that carry weight where it belongs.

This law does not call for less action. It calls for more precision.

Every intervention should answer a second question: where has the load gone now?

If that question cannot be answered, the organisation is accruing debt it does not yet see.

And unseen debt is always the most expensive kind.

Law 3: Complexity Always Outruns Culture

Culture is often treated as a stabiliser.

Shared values. Trusted norms. A common way of working. In early stages of growth, culture performs this role well. It fills gaps. It guides behaviour when rules are unclear. It allows people to act with confidence in ambiguous situations.

At scale, this stops working.

Complexity always outruns culture.

This is not a critique of culture. It is a recognition of its limits. Culture operates through shared understanding. Complexity fragments that understanding by multiplying interfaces, decisions, and dependencies. The more complex the organisation becomes, the less uniformly culture can be applied.

Culture cannot compensate for missing decision rights.

When authority is unclear, culture encourages caution. People defer. They seek alignment. They avoid risk. These behaviours are often praised as collaborative or respectful. Under scale, they slow execution.

The organisation appears polite but hesitant.

Decisions that should be resolved locally are escalated. Ownership diffuses. Accountability blurs. Culture does not resolve this. It masks it.

People behave well while waiting.

Culture also cannot compensate for broken process flow.

Processes define how work moves. Culture influences how people feel about moving it. When flow is poorly designed, culture fills the gap temporarily through goodwill and effort. People go the extra mile. They coordinate informally. They adapt.

As volume increases, this adaptation becomes unsustainable.

Good intentions do not unblock queues. Shared values do not remove handoffs. Alignment does not replace sequencing. The organisation works harder to maintain momentum, but momentum degrades.

This is often misinterpreted as a need to reinforce culture.

Leaders invest in engagement. They communicate values. They run workshops. Morale improves briefly. Flow does not.

The problem is not attitude. It is architecture.

Role clarity follows the same pattern.

In small teams, roles can be fluid. People help where needed. Culture supports this flexibility. As the organisation grows, fluidity becomes ambiguity. Overlap increases. Gaps appear. Responsibility is shared without ownership.

Culture encourages people to be helpful. It does not define who decides.

At scale, this becomes dangerous.

Work falls between roles. Decisions are delayed. Conflicts are managed rather than resolved. Leaders step in to arbitrate. The organisation remains civil, but slow.

Culture cannot absorb this load.

The critical misunderstanding is believing that strong culture scales automatically.

It does not.

Culture spreads through proximity, repetition, and reinforcement. As organisations grow, proximity decreases. Messages dilute. Interpretations diverge. Subcultures form. The organisation becomes plural.

This is not failure. It is physics.

Complexity introduces variation faster than culture can standardise behaviour. The organisation fragments while believing it is aligned.

This is why leaders often feel surprised when cultural issues appear in successful organisations. They invested heavily. They communicated clearly. They modelled values. The culture seemed strong.

What changed was scale.

The same culture that enabled early success becomes insufficient to coordinate a larger system. It cannot resolve the increased number of decisions, interactions, and trade offs. It lacks the precision required under load.

This does not mean culture becomes irrelevant. It means its role changes.

Culture sets intent. Structure enables execution.

Without structure, culture becomes a source of frustration. People care. They want to do the right thing. They are constrained by ambiguity. Over time, this gap erodes trust.

Leaders then face a paradox.

They believe culture is the answer, so they reinforce it. The organisation responds emotionally, but not operationally. Execution does not improve. Pressure increases.

Eventually, culture is blamed for problems it cannot solve.

This is unfair and counterproductive.

Culture did not fail. It was overextended.

Once complexity reaches a certain threshold, only design can coordinate behaviour reliably. Decision rights must be explicit. Process flow must be engineered. Roles must be clear enough to act without permission.

Culture supports these elements. It cannot replace them.

This is why high growth organisations often experience a cultural dip.

Not because values were lost, but because structure lagged. People are asked to uphold standards in systems that do not support them. The strain is misattributed to attitude.

The result is cynicism.

People hear values but experience friction. They are told to take ownership but lack authority. They are encouraged to collaborate but punished for delay. Culture becomes rhetoric rather than reality.

This is avoidable.

When structure is designed to carry complexity, culture regains its proper role. It shapes how people behave within clear boundaries. It reinforces good decisions rather than compensating for missing ones.

The law is simple.

Culture amplifies structure. It cannot replace it.

As complexity increases, the organisation must rely less on shared assumptions and more on explicit design. This is not bureaucracy. It is clarity.

Leaders who cling to culture as a primary coordination mechanism under scale create frustration. Leaders who redesign decision rights, flow, and roles allow culture to do what it does best.

Complexity will always outrun culture.

The choice is whether structure keeps pace.

When it does, culture remains a strength.

When it does not, culture is asked to carry weight it was never meant to bear.

And no amount of values can hold a system together once that threshold is crossed.

Law 4: The Bottleneck Is Usually a Decision, Not a Person

When progress slows, organisations look for people to fix.

The wrong hire. The underperforming manager. The team that cannot keep up. Capability becomes the default explanation because it is tangible. Individuals can be assessed, replaced, or coached. Action feels possible.

Most of the time, this diagnosis is wrong.

The bottleneck is usually a decision, not a person.

People appear to be the constraint because they are where the constraint surfaces. Work waits on them. Approvals queue with them. Issues escalate to them. From the outside, it looks like overload or indecision. From a structural perspective, it is misrouted authority.

Leaders blame capability when decisions are poorly designed.

A manager hesitates because the decision sits in a grey zone. They are accountable for the outcome but lack authority to decide. Escalation feels safer than action. Delay follows. The person appears cautious. The system is ambiguous.

Another leader becomes a bottleneck because too many decisions flow through them. Not because they want control, but because the organisation has no other resolution path. Their judgement substitutes for design. They are constantly involved. Their availability limits throughput.

This is not a capability issue. It is a routing problem.

Decisions slow when authority design is unclear.

Authority is not about hierarchy. It is about permission matched to responsibility. When those two are misaligned, decisions stall. People wait for confirmation. Escalation becomes routine. The organisation moves cautiously, even when confident people are present.

Under scale, this misalignment compounds.

Each additional layer adds more interfaces. Each interface introduces uncertainty. Without explicit decision rights, ambiguity multiplies. The organisation defaults to escalation to manage risk.

This is how decision congestion forms.

Sequencing matters just as much.

Many organisations ask people to decide without providing sequence. Priorities conflict. Dependencies are unclear. Decisions are made out of order. Work must be revisited. Rework increases. Frustration follows.

From the outside, it looks like poor judgement.

In reality, people are deciding in a system that does not tell them what must be resolved first. They are reacting rather than progressing. No amount of capability can compensate for missing sequence.

Escalation paths complete the picture.

When escalation is undefined, everything escalates. When escalation is too easy, it replaces ownership. When escalation is too hard, risk is hidden. In all cases, the decision bottleneck shifts upward.

Leaders become the constraint not because they are slow, but because they are absorbing decisions that should not reach them.

This absorption feels responsible. It is destructive.

The organisation learns that progress requires senior attention. Initiative narrows. People wait. Leaders intervene more. The system reinforces the bottleneck it complains about.

Blaming people at this stage is convenient.

It avoids redesign. It preserves the illusion that replacing individuals will restore speed. Sometimes replacing a person provides temporary relief. The structure remains unchanged. The bottleneck reappears.

This cycle is common.

High performers are promoted into overloaded roles. They cope for a while. The organisation praises their reliability. Eventually, they slow. The organisation concludes they have reached their limit.

The limit was never personal. It was structural.

Understanding this law changes how leaders interpret friction.

Instead of asking who is blocking progress, they ask where decisions are stalling and why. They examine authority boundaries. They clarify sequence. They redesign escalation paths.

When this is done, something unexpected happens.

The same people move faster.

Managers who appeared hesitant act decisively. Leaders who were overloaded regain time. Teams that seemed dependent operate independently. Performance improves without changing talent.

This is not transformation. It is correction.

The organisation stops asking individuals to resolve ambiguity the system should have removed.

This law is uncomfortable because it removes a familiar lever. Leaders can no longer fix speed by replacing people alone. They must redesign how decisions are made.

It also restores fairness.

People are no longer blamed for behaving rationally in poorly designed systems. Accountability becomes meaningful because authority is real. Performance improves because flow improves.

Most bottlenecks are decisions waiting for clarity.

Once clarity exists, the bottleneck disappears without drama.

This is why great organisations are not staffed with extraordinary people everywhere. They are designed so that ordinary decisions do not require extraordinary effort.

When leaders stop confusing people with constraints, they stop treating symptoms and start addressing causes.

The organisation becomes faster not by demanding more, but by deciding better.

And better decisions come from design, not from pressure placed on individuals.

This law completes a critical shift.

If the bottleneck is a decision, then removing it requires architecture. Not motivation. Not capability uplift. Not heroic leadership.

Just clear authority, proper sequence, and disciplined escalation.

When those are in place, people rarely slow the organisation down.

They simply do what the system finally allows them to do.

Law 5: Greatness Is Proven by Transferability

Greatness is often mistaken for performance under ideal conditions.

Strong leaders present. Key individuals engaged. Experience concentrated where it matters. Under these circumstances, many organisations perform exceptionally well. Results arrive. Pressure is absorbed. The organisation appears robust.

This is not proof of greatness.

Greatness is proven when performance transfers.

Transferability is the organisation's ability to produce outcomes independent of specific individuals. It is the capacity to sustain direction, value creation, and momentum when leaders step back, move roles, or exit entirely.

If performance collapses when certain people are absent, the organisation is not great. It is dependent.

Dependency is easily confused with strength.

Charismatic founders. Tireless executives. Exceptional operators. Their presence stabilises the organisation. Their judgement resolves ambiguity. Their relationships unblock issues. Performance holds because they are there.

The organisation learns to rely on them.

From the inside, this feels like leadership. From a structural view, it is fragility being masked by competence.

Transferability exposes the difference.

In a transferable organisation, outcomes persist even as individuals change. Knowledge is embedded. Authority is clear. Decisions move through defined paths. Systems carry routine load. Leaders are replaceable without destabilising flow.

In a dependent organisation, outcomes are personal.

Decisions require specific people. Context lives in heads rather than structure. Authority is informal. Systems are incomplete. When key individuals are unavailable, progress slows or stops.

The organisation functions, but only conditionally.

This conditionality is rarely visible during stability.

As long as the right people remain engaged, dependency feels manageable. Leaders interpret reliance as trust. Involvement feels necessary. The organisation adapts around its strongest performers.

The cost is hidden until change occurs.

Leadership transition is the most common test.

When a senior leader steps back, takes leave, or moves on, the organisation experiences disruption disproportionate to the change. Decisions stall. Priorities blur. Momentum drops. The gap between documented process and lived reality becomes obvious.

This is not because the successor is incapable. It is because the organisation was never designed to function without the predecessor.

Another test is growth.

As the organisation expands, leaders cannot be everywhere. Dependency becomes a constraint. Scale stalls because judgement cannot be replicated. The organisation slows not due to lack of opportunity, but because it cannot transfer responsibility safely.

At this point, leaders often attempt delegation.

Delegation fails when transferability is absent.

Work is handed off, but authority is not. Responsibility is assigned, but decision rights remain unclear. Leaders continue to intervene to ensure outcomes. Delegation becomes supervision. Supervision becomes exhaustion.

The organisation concludes that delegation is risky.

The real issue is design.

Transferability requires deliberate architecture.

Decisions must be explicit enough to move without interpretation. Systems must carry context so it does not have to be remembered.

Roles must be defined so ownership is clear. Cadence must reinforce priorities consistently.

Without these elements, individuals remain load bearing.

Greatness that depends on individuals is temporary.

It lasts as long as those individuals are present, healthy, and willing to carry the weight. It does not survive transition, growth, or sustained pressure.

This is why many organisations plateau after initial success.

They are excellent at execution under supervision. They are weak at execution without it. Leaders feel trapped because stepping back creates risk. Growth increases dependency rather than reducing it.

This is not leadership failure. It is architectural incompleteness.

Transferability also reframes succession.

Succession planning often focuses on identifying the next leader. In a dependent organisation, succession is dangerous regardless of who follows. The system requires the person it lost.

In a transferable organisation, succession is uneventful.

The organisation notices the change. It adjusts. Performance continues. This is not because individuals are interchangeable, but because the structure supports continuity.

This distinction matters because it defines what greatness actually is.

Greatness is not the presence of exceptional individuals. It is the absence of dependence on them.

This does not diminish leadership. It elevates it.

Leaders who design for transferability create organisations that outlast them. Leaders who do not remain essential to their own success.

The law is uncompromising.

If the organisation cannot perform without specific individuals, it is not great. It is dependent.

This dependence may be masked by loyalty, effort, and commitment. It may persist for years. It will eventually be exposed by change.

Leaders who understand this law stop measuring success by how involved they are. They measure it by how unnecessary their involvement has become.

Not because they are disengaged, but because the organisation can carry itself.

Transferability is the final proof.

It demonstrates that structure, not heroics, is doing the work. It shows that capacity exists beyond individuals. It confirms that greatness is embedded, not performed.

Everything else can be impressive.

Only this is durable.

CHAPTER 6:
The Greatness Audit, What to Measure Before You Move

The 3XV Diagnostic, Clarity Test in One Page

Most organisations believe they are clear.

They have articulated vision. They understand their value proposition. They know how they go to market. These elements are documented, communicated, and often revisited. From the inside, clarity feels present.

The problem is that stated clarity and operational clarity are not the same thing.

The purpose of this diagnostic is not to evaluate ambition. It is to expose alignment. Specifically, whether direction, value creation, and movement are reinforcing one another structurally, or merely coexisting rhetorically.

This distinction matters because misalignment does not announce itself as confusion. It presents as effort.

When direction, value, and movement are aligned, the organisation feels coherent under pressure. When they are not, effort increases without corresponding leverage.

The first element to examine is direction.

Direction is not what leaders say. It is what the organisation consistently prioritises when trade offs are required.

Many organisations have a clear vision statement. Fewer have a clear directional mechanism. Direction becomes diluted when priorities compete and there is no structural cadence to resolve conflict.

The diagnostic question is simple.

When priorities clash, what actually decides?

If direction is aligned, decisions resolve consistently across the organisation. Teams make similar trade offs independently. Escalation is rare because intent is operationalised, not just stated.

If direction is merely stated, trade offs are negotiated repeatedly. Decisions escalate. Meetings are required to align interpretation. Leaders are asked to arbitrate.

The signal is not disagreement. It is dependency.

Aligned direction reduces dependency. Stated direction increases it.

The second element is value.

Value is not what the organisation claims to deliver. It is what it can deliver reliably, repeatedly, and at scale.

Many organisations articulate value clearly. The issue is flow.

When value creation is aligned with direction, work moves predictably from intent to outcome. Bottlenecks are known. Exceptions are visible. Quality is consistent.

When value is misaligned, delivery becomes variable. Some initiatives succeed, others stall. Outcomes depend on who is involved rather than on how the system operates. Leaders intervene to protect standards.

The diagnostic question here is not about customer satisfaction. It is about predictability.

Can the organisation forecast outcomes with confidence, or does it rely on last minute coordination to deliver?

Aligned value shows up as stability. Misaligned value shows up as volatility.

The third element is movement.

Movement is the organisation's ability to progress initiatives without constant intervention. It is not speed for its own sake. It is continuity.

When movement is aligned, initiatives advance through defined stages. Dependencies are managed structurally. Progress continues even when leaders are absent.

When movement is misaligned, progress is episodic. Initiatives surge under attention and stall without it. Priorities shift frequently. The organisation is busy, but not always advancing.

The diagnostic question is this.

Does progress require presence?

If leaders must remain closely involved to maintain momentum, movement is not structurally supported. If progress continues without constant oversight, movement is embedded.

Aligned movement reduces leadership load. Misaligned movement concentrates it.

The power of this diagnostic lies in examining these elements together.

Direction without aligned value creates frustration. Teams know what matters, but cannot deliver consistently. Effort increases. Confidence declines.

Value without aligned movement creates instability. The organisation can deliver, but only through bursts of attention. Leaders feel indispensable. Scale feels risky.

Movement without aligned direction creates chaos. Work progresses, but not coherently. Resources are consumed without clear impact. Strategy feels disconnected from execution.

When all three are aligned, something distinct emerges.

The organisation feels calm under pressure. Decisions resolve without escalation. Work moves without drama. Leaders are informed rather than required. Performance holds without exhaustion.

This state is rare not because it is complex, but because misalignment is hard to see from inside.

Organisations often assess these elements independently.

They review strategy. They analyse value propositions. They track project progress. Each assessment may be positive. Alignment between them is assumed rather than tested.

This diagnostic collapses that assumption.

It asks leaders to observe behaviour rather than intention. To examine what happens under load rather than what is planned. To notice where effort increases rather than where results appear.

Importantly, this is not a scoring exercise.

The output is not a number. It is a pattern.

Where decisions escalate, direction is not operationalised. Where delivery varies, value is not flowing. Where progress depends on intervention, movement is not structured.

These signals appear before performance declines. They are early indicators of architectural strain.

The diagnostic can be completed quickly because it relies on lived experience.

Leaders know where they are involved. Middle managers know where work stalls. Teams know where clarity breaks down. The answers are present. They are rarely connected.

This is why the diagnostic fits on one page.

Its purpose is not analysis. It is orientation.

It shows whether the organisation is attempting to scale on intent or on design. Whether clarity exists structurally or rhetorically. Whether effort is being used to compensate for misalignment.

If direction, value, and movement are aligned, the organisation is ready to move.

If they are not, moving faster will only amplify strain.

This is the point of measurement before action.

Not to delay change, but to sequence it. Not to debate strategy, but to locate constraint. Not to motivate, but to reveal.

The diagnostic does not tell leaders what to do next. It tells them whether the organisation can carry what it is already trying to do.

That insight alone changes behaviour.

Because once misalignment is seen, it cannot be unseen.

And when alignment is present, effort finally produces leverage instead of fatigue.

This is the clarity test.

Not of ambition, but of architecture.

Pillar Baselines, What "Strong" Actually Means

Most organisations believe they know whether they are strong.

They point to results, growth, talent, or reputation. These indicators describe performance. They do not describe capacity. Strength, in an architectural sense, is not about how well something works when supported. It is about whether it carries load without distortion.

Baselines exist to answer a simpler question.

Can the organisation carry its current weight without compensating effort?

Each pillar represents a different load path. None can be assessed in isolation. A weakness in one is often hidden by strength in another. The purpose of baselines is not scoring. It is exposure.

A pillar is strong when it absorbs pressure quietly.

A pillar is at risk when pressure produces workarounds.

The first pillar concerns how work is structured.

A strong baseline is visible when work flows without constant clarification. Processes are understood well enough to act without interpretation. Exceptions are genuinely exceptional. People do not need to ask how work should move, they know.

Risk appears when work requires explanation. When process exists but is bypassed. When individuals hold unofficial versions of how things really get done. The organisation relies on memory, not structure.

Pass looks like flow.

Risk looks like dependency.

The second pillar concerns who does the work and how roles are aligned.

A strong baseline exists when roles are clear enough that ownership is obvious. People know what they are responsible for and what they are not. Capability matches responsibility. Handoffs are intentional, not negotiated.

Risk appears when responsibility is broad but authority is conditional. When people are accountable without permission. When escalation is frequent because roles are unclear. The organisation compensates by relying on experience rather than clarity.

Pass looks like confidence.

Risk looks like hesitation.

The third pillar concerns how growth is handled.

A strong baseline exists when growth does not concentrate load. As volume increases, decisions distribute rather than centralise. Leaders are not pulled deeper into execution. The organisation expands without increasing fragility.

Risk appears when growth amplifies dependency. When leaders become more essential as the organisation gets bigger. When scale increases coordination faster than output. The organisation grows, but becomes harder to run.

Pass looks like leverage.

Risk looks like saturation.

The fourth pillar concerns endurance.

A strong baseline exists when the organisation can sustain performance without exhausting people. Pressure reveals issues early. Recovery is built in. Leaders retain time to think. Teams can maintain pace without constant urgency.

Risk appears when performance is protected through heroics. When pressure is absorbed by individuals. When exhaustion is normalised. The organisation survives, but at a cost that compounds.

Pass looks like stability.

Risk looks like strain.

The fifth pillar concerns transferability.

A strong baseline exists when outcomes do not depend on specific individuals. Knowledge is embedded. Decisions travel through structure. Succession is uneventful. Delegation does not create risk.

Risk appears when absence creates disruption. When leaders cannot step back without anxiety. When delegation requires supervision. The organisation works because certain people are present.

Pass looks like continuity.

Risk looks like reliance.

These baselines are intentionally simple.

They are not benchmarks against other organisations. They are internal tests. Each asks whether strength is structural or personal. Whether success is carried by design or by effort.

Importantly, most organisations will pass some baselines and fail others.

That is normal.

Risk is rarely evenly distributed. Strong systems can hide weak staffing. Strong leaders can hide weak process. Strong culture can hide weak decision design. Baselines reveal where compensation is occurring.

This is why results alone are misleading.

An organisation may appear strong because people are absorbing load across multiple pillars. The baselines show where that absorption is happening and whether it is sustainable.

Pass does not mean perfect. It means resilient.

Risk does not mean failure. It means fragility.

Leaders often discover that their organisation is strong in the areas they personally oversee and at risk where they are less visible. This is not coincidence. It reflects where attention has been compensating for design.

The value of baselines is not in labelling. It is in sequencing.

They show where redesign will produce leverage and where it will simply add noise. They indicate which issues are upstream and which are symptoms. They prevent the organisation from treating visible pain while ignoring invisible load.

Baselines also change the conversation.

Instead of debating whether something is good enough, leaders ask whether it is load bearing. Instead of celebrating effort, they examine strain. Instead of assuming strength, they test it.

This reframing removes emotion.

The organisation is not criticised. It is measured. Not against ideals, but against reality. The baselines describe what is, not what should be.

That clarity is uncomfortable and grounding.

It allows leaders to move from intuition to architecture. To see where strength is real and where it is being simulated through effort.

Only then does change become precise.

Because what is strong does not need fixing.

What is at risk does not need motivation.

It needs design.

The Load Map, Where the Weight Is Really Sitting

Most organisations underestimate where work actually happens.

They track outputs, milestones, and responsibilities. They review performance and capacity through formal structures. What they rarely map is load, the invisible weight being carried to keep the system functioning.

Load is not evenly distributed. It accumulates where structure is weak.

The purpose of a load map is not to catalogue tasks. It is to reveal compensation. To show where effort is substituting for design and where weight is being carried informally rather than structurally.

The first place load hides is meetings.

Meetings absorb work when decisions cannot move on their own. Each meeting represents unresolved authority, unclear priorities, or broken flow. They are not inherently wasteful. They are adaptive.

When meetings increase without corresponding clarity, they are carrying load.

Recurring alignment sessions indicate that direction is not embedded. Escalation meetings signal unclear decision rights. Status updates replace flow when progress cannot be trusted without supervision.

The load map asks a simple question.

If this meeting did not exist, what would break?

If the answer is decision making, authority is missing. If the answer is coordination, flow is broken. If the answer is confidence, trust has been replaced by oversight.

Meetings are the most visible form of invisible load.

The second concentration point is approvals.

Approvals accumulate where risk is unmanaged by design. When authority is unclear, decisions move upward. When consequences are asymmetric, people seek protection. Approval chains grow.

Each approval appears reasonable. Collectively, they slow the organisation.

Approvals are load because they consume attention and delay action. They shift responsibility upward and concentrate decision making at the top. Leaders become throughput rather than designers.

The load map does not ask how many approvals exist. It asks why they are required.

Are approvals protecting quality, or compensating for unclear accountability?

Are they exceptional, or routine?

Do they resolve risk, or merely redistribute it?

Routine approvals indicate that the organisation does not trust its own structure to carry decisions.

The third area is exceptions.

Exceptions are often celebrated as flexibility. They allow the organisation to respond to nuance and opportunity. Used sparingly, they are healthy.

When exceptions become common, they are load.

Each exception bypasses structure. It requires judgement, coordination, and often senior involvement. The organisation adapts, but the system weakens. What was once exceptional becomes expected.

The load map looks for patterns.

Which rules are regularly bypassed?

Which processes require "special handling"?

Which customers, products, or teams operate outside the norm?

Exceptions reveal where the architecture cannot accommodate reality. They are signals, not irritations.

The fourth and most dangerous load carrier is hero performers.

Hero performers are individuals who consistently make things work. They anticipate issues. They know who to call. They bridge gaps. They absorb complexity without complaint.

They are often praised.

From a structural perspective, they are load bearing.

When outcomes depend on specific people, the organisation is compensating. Knowledge is tacit. Flow is personal. Risk is concentrated.

The load map identifies where heroics are required.

Which individuals are always involved when things get difficult?

Who is copied on everything "just in case"?

Who cannot take time off without disruption?

These patterns are not evidence of excellence. They are evidence of missing design.

Importantly, load is rarely visible where it originates.

A weak process creates load in meetings.

An unclear role creates load in approvals.

A fragile system creates load in people.

This is why organisations struggle to locate the source of strain. They feel pressure in one area, but the cause sits elsewhere.

The load map reverses the view.

Instead of asking where work is hard, it asks where effort is compensating. Instead of optimising visible pain points, it traces weight back to structural gaps.

This is uncomfortable because it challenges familiar narratives.

Meetings are not a communication problem.

Approvals are not a control problem.

Heroics are not a talent problem.

They are design problems.

The value of the load map is not diagnosis alone. It is restraint.

Once leaders see where load is being carried informally, they stop adding weight elsewhere. They stop introducing new initiatives that increase meetings. They stop layering approvals to manage risk. They stop rewarding heroics without questioning necessity.

They begin to remove load deliberately.

This does not mean eliminating meetings, approvals, or exceptional effort entirely. It means restoring them to their proper role.

Meetings become decision points, not holding areas.

Approvals become safeguards, not defaults.

Exceptional effort becomes rare again.

The organisation becomes lighter without becoming lax.

The load map also changes leadership behaviour.

Leaders notice where their presence is required and ask why. They identify where they are the system and design themselves out of it. They stop absorbing load reflexively and start interpreting it.

This shift is subtle but powerful.

The organisation learns that strain is information, not a test of commitment. People stop compensating silently. Signals surface earlier. Redesign becomes possible before exhaustion sets in.

The load map is not a document. It is a perspective.

It teaches leaders to see beyond formal structures and into lived reality. To notice where effort is being spent to make the system work and to ask what the system should be doing instead.

Once seen, invisible load is difficult to ignore.

Because it explains why the organisation feels heavy even when results are strong.

And it shows precisely where design, not effort, must change next.

The Drift Scan, Where "Fine" Is Quietly Becoming Fragile

Drift does not announce itself as failure.

It appears as "fine".

Operations are stable. People are committed. Customers are satisfied. Margins are acceptable. Decisions are being made. From the outside, there is no obvious reason to intervene. From the inside, something feels off, but not urgent.

This is the most dangerous state an organisation can be in.

The purpose of a drift scan is not to identify problems. It is to detect weakening signals before they are reclassified as crises. Drift is not about decline. It is about misalignment slowly widening under continued performance.

Drift always appears first at the edges.

The first area is operations.

Operational drift shows up as increasing variability. Processes still work, but not consistently. Delivery depends more on who is involved than on how the work is designed. Exceptions increase quietly. Teams develop their own ways of handling similar tasks.

Nothing breaks. Reliability erodes.

From the inside, this is described as nuance. From a structural view, it is loss of standard flow. Operations become harder to predict. Planning becomes more cautious. Buffers are added to compensate.

Operational drift is present when effort rises but output does not.

The second area is people.

People drift is not disengagement. It is narrowing.

High performers become protective of their time. Initiative contracts. Risk tolerance drops. People stop challenging decisions that feel ambiguous because doing so costs energy. The organisation remains polite, but less curious.

This is often misread as maturity.

In reality, people are adapting to friction. They are conserving bandwidth in a system that demands constant compensation. Commitment remains, but ambition becomes selective.

The signal is subtle.

People do what is asked. They stop doing what is possible.

The third area is customers.

Customer drift does not begin with complaints. It begins with reduced surprise.

The organisation still delivers. Customers still buy. What fades is differentiation. Response times lengthen slightly. Innovation slows. Interactions become transactional rather than distinctive.

Customers adjust expectations quietly.

This is rarely visible in headline metrics. Retention remains stable. Revenue holds. The organisation assumes loyalty.

In reality, the relationship is becoming fragile. When alternatives appear, switching becomes easier because emotional and operational differentiation has thinned.

Customer drift is present when satisfaction remains but advocacy declines.

The fourth area is margins.

Margin drift is often explained externally.

Input costs rise. Competition increases. Pricing pressure intensifies. These explanations may be accurate, but they obscure an internal shift.

As drift sets in, the cost of coordination increases. More time is spent managing complexity. More people are involved in delivery. More exceptions are handled manually. Margins compress not because value declined, but because effort increased.

This compression feels manageable.

Leaders adjust targets. They optimise costs. They accept slightly lower returns as the price of scale. What is missed is that the organisation is paying interest on structural debt.

Margin drift is present when cost control requires constant attention.

The fifth and most telling area is decision speed.

Decision drift is rarely framed as a problem. Slower decisions are justified as being thoughtful, inclusive, or prudent. Leaders take pride in deliberation. Risk management appears strong.

The question is not how carefully decisions are made. It is how long they take relative to the environment.

When decision speed slows incrementally, opportunities narrow. Initiatives miss windows. Competitors move first. The organisation responds, but later.

Decision drift is present when timing becomes the limiting factor rather than quality.

These indicators do not appear simultaneously. They accumulate unevenly.

Operations may feel heavy before customers notice. People may narrow before margins compress. Decision speed may decline while results still hold. This staggered pattern makes drift hard to see.

Each signal is explainable in isolation. Together, they form a trajectory.

The defining characteristic of drift is that it feels reasonable.

Leaders adapt. Teams adjust. The organisation compensates. Performance remains acceptable. There is no obvious moment that demands action.

This is why drift persists.

The drift scan is not about judgement. It is about honesty.

It asks leaders to observe where "fine" is being upheld by effort rather than carried by design. Where stability depends on attention rather than structure. Where adaptation has become normal.

The scan does not ask whether the organisation is succeeding.

It asks whether success is becoming heavier to sustain.

When multiple drift signals appear, the organisation is already fragile, even if it does not yet feel vulnerable. The system is working harder to stay in place.

This is the final warning before optionality narrows.

Drift does not force change. It invites explanation. Organisations that drift rarely panic. They rationalise. They optimise. They wait.

By the time drift becomes visible as decline, the opportunity to redesign calmly has passed.

The value of the drift scan is timing.

It allows leaders to act while pressure is still informative rather than destructive. To redesign before compensation becomes dependence. To restore capacity before exhaustion sets in.

Drift is not failure in progress.

It is architecture falling slightly behind reality.

The earlier it is seen, the lighter the correction.

The later it is acknowledged, the heavier the cost.

This scan exists to make the invisible visible while choice still exists.

Because "fine" is not neutral.

It is often the last stable state before fragility becomes unavoidable.

CHAPTER 7
The 90-Day Rebuild Plan, Clarity, Capacity, Cadence

Days 1 to 15, Stop the Bleeding Without Cosmetic Change

The first fifteen days are not about improvement.

They are about containment.

When organisations finally acknowledge structural strain, the instinct is to act visibly. Announce change. Signal momentum. Reassure stakeholders. Launch initiatives that demonstrate control.

This instinct is understandable and dangerous.

Early visibility creates noise before clarity exists. It triggers behavioural response before structural understanding. The organisation begins adapting to an intervention that has not yet been designed.

The first phase is deliberately quiet.

Its purpose is to stop further damage while preserving what still works. To prevent well intentioned action from increasing load. To create the conditions for accurate redesign.

The first decision is what to freeze.

Freezing is not inactivity. It is restraint.

In the opening days, leaders pause non essential change. New initiatives are delayed. Process upgrades are suspended. Structural experiments are put on hold. This includes well meaning programmes that promise quick wins.

Each additional change during this period adds variables. It obscures signals. It increases coordination cost at precisely the moment clarity is required.

Freezing creates a stable reference point.

It allows leaders to observe where pressure already exists rather than introducing new sources of strain. It prevents the organisation from compensating further while diagnosis is underway.

Importantly, freezing is selective.

Critical customer facing work continues. Safety, compliance, and core delivery are protected. The freeze applies to discretionary change, not operational continuity.

This distinction matters because it signals seriousness without panic.

The second decision is what to protect.

Protection is about preserving capacity that will be needed for redesign.

Certain individuals, teams, and rhythms are already overloaded. They are absorbing load informally. They are the shock absorbers of the system. During early intervention, these areas must be shielded from additional demands.

Leaders identify where heroics are occurring and prevent further extraction.

This may feel counterintuitive. When pressure is visible, organisations often lean harder on their most reliable performers. In this phase, that impulse is reversed.

Protection buys time.

It prevents burnout. It preserves institutional knowledge. It ensures that those who understand the system best are not exhausted before redesign begins.

Protection also applies to decision space.

Leaders protect thinking time. They reduce meeting volume where possible. They resist the urge to fill silence with activity. This creates cognitive capacity to interpret what is being seen.

The third decision is what not to announce.

This is often the hardest.

Leaders feel obligated to explain. To reassure. To demonstrate action. Announcements satisfy emotional needs, but they create expectations the organisation will immediately begin adapting to.

In the first fifteen days, most announcements are premature.

The organisation does not yet know what will change. Signalling direction before design exists invites speculation, resistance, and misalignment. People begin optimising around assumptions. Load increases.

Silence, used intentionally, is stabilising.

This does not mean secrecy. It means discretion.

Leaders communicate boundaries, not solutions. They explain that certain changes are paused. They reinforce priorities that remain unchanged. They avoid promising outcomes.

The message is containment, not transformation.

This creates psychological safety without triggering adaptation.

During this phase, leaders observe rather than intervene.

They watch where work queues. Where decisions stall. Where escalations occur. They note which meetings feel essential and which exist to manage uncertainty. They pay attention to where they are personally required.

This observation is not passive.

It is disciplined.

Leaders resist the urge to solve what they see. They allow friction to surface long enough to understand its source. They distinguish between noise and signal.

This is difficult because leaders are accustomed to relieving pressure. In this phase, relieving pressure too quickly destroys information.

The goal is not to let the organisation suffer. It is to let the system speak.

Another critical action in this period is removing cosmetic change.

Cosmetic change alters appearance without affecting load. Rebranding initiatives. Structural reshuffles without authority redesign. New reporting formats that do not change decisions. These actions create activity while leaving architecture untouched.

Cosmetic change is seductive because it produces visible motion. It reassures stakeholders that something is happening. It also consumes capacity that is needed for real redesign.

In the first fifteen days, cosmetic change is actively resisted.

Leaders test proposals with a simple question.

Does this reduce load, or does it rearrange it?

If the answer is unclear, the change waits.

This discipline prevents the organisation from mistaking movement for progress.

During this period, leaders also establish a temporary operating posture.

Escalation thresholds are raised. Not eliminated, but clarified. Leaders make it explicit that only true exceptions should reach them. This creates space to see where escalation is structural rather than habitual.

They do not punish escalation. They examine it.

Each escalation is treated as data. Why did this arrive here? What prevented resolution below? What design element is missing?

This posture shifts the organisation subtly.

People sense that intervention is no longer automatic. They begin to reflect on authority. Some decisions slow briefly. That slowdown is informative.

This is why the phase must be short.

Fifteen days is enough to reveal patterns without allowing drift to worsen. Longer freezes create anxiety. Shorter periods do not surface signal.

By the end of this phase, leaders should not have answers.

They should have clarity.

Clarity about where load is concentrated. About which parts of the organisation are compensating. About which behaviours are adaptive responses to design gaps rather than performance issues.

They should see the organisation more accurately than before.

This is the only success criterion for the first fifteen days.

Not momentum.

Not morale.

Not visible improvement.

Accuracy.

Without this containment phase, every subsequent action risks reinforcing the very patterns it intends to fix. The organisation will adapt around change rather than being redesigned by it.

Stopping the bleeding is not dramatic.

It is disciplined restraint.

It signals that the organisation will no longer trade long term capacity for short term relief. That it will observe before acting. That it understands the cost of premature certainty.

This tone sets everything that follows.

Because once the system is no longer compensating reflexively, the real work can begin.

Not with noise.

But with precision.

Days 16 to 30, Decision Architecture Reset

Once the system has been stabilised, attention shifts to the primary constraint.

Decisions.

In most organisations under strain, decisions are not absent. They are misrouted. They arrive late, incomplete, or escalated by default. Effort has been compensating for unclear authority, broken sequence, and informal escalation.

This phase resets that architecture quietly and deliberately.

The objective is not speed. It is correctness of flow.

The first focus is decision rights.

Decision rights are often implied rather than defined. Job titles suggest authority. Experience fills gaps. Escalation resolves uncertainty. This works at low scale. Under load, it collapses.

During this phase, leaders clarify three things only.

Who decides.

What they decide.

What happens when they decide.

This is not a governance exercise. It is a load redistribution exercise.

Decisions that are currently escalated are examined one by one. Not to judge competence, but to locate ambiguity. If a decision requires senior involvement, the question is why. Is the risk unclear. Is the outcome reversible. Is accountability misaligned.

Wherever possible, authority is pushed back down with explicit permission. Not vague empowerment, but bounded authority. People are told what they can decide without asking and what requires escalation.

This clarity immediately reduces load.

People stop hesitating. Leaders stop absorbing decisions unnecessarily. Flow improves without changing headcount or strategy.

The second focus is escalation paths.

Escalation is not failure. It is a design feature. When escalation is undefined, everything escalates. When it is too rigid, risk is hidden.

In this phase, escalation is made explicit.

Leaders define what qualifies as an exception. They clarify thresholds. They specify where issues should go first and when they should move upward.

This removes ambiguity.

People no longer escalate to be safe. They escalate because the situation genuinely requires senior judgement. The volume of escalation drops. The quality improves.

Importantly, leaders resist the urge to intervene outside these paths. When they do intervene, they explain why. This reinforces the new architecture rather than undermining it.

The third focus is meeting purpose.

Meetings are redesigned as decision mechanisms, not information exchanges.

Every recurring meeting is examined with a single question.

What decision does this meeting exist to make.

If there is no clear answer, the meeting is carrying load that should sit elsewhere. It is paused, shortened, or repurposed.

Meetings that remain are given explicit decision rights. Attendees know what they are expected to resolve. Preparation shifts from updates to options. Outcomes are defined.

This change is subtle but powerful.

Meetings become fewer. They also become more consequential. Time is reclaimed not by cancellation alone, but by clarity.

The organisation begins to feel lighter because decisions move without looping.

The fourth focus is reporting.

Reporting often exists to provide comfort rather than action. Dashboards are reviewed. Metrics are tracked. Conversations repeat. Decisions are deferred.

In this phase, reporting is redesigned to force choice.

Reports that do not lead to a decision are deprioritised. Data is framed around variance, risk, and trade offs. Leaders ask fewer questions about performance and more about constraint.

Reporting becomes directional.

Instead of asking what happened, it asks what must change. Instead of reviewing everything, it highlights what requires action. This reduces cognitive load and accelerates resolution.

The organisation learns that reporting is not about visibility. It is about movement.

Throughout this phase, leaders maintain restraint.

They do not announce a transformation. They do not roll out new frameworks. They do not rename roles. They adjust the mechanics of decision making quietly and consistently.

The effect is immediate.

Middle management feels relief. They can act without constant validation. Teams experience clarity. Leaders notice fewer interruptions.

Importantly, this phase reveals gaps.

Some decisions cannot be reassigned because capability is missing. Some escalations persist because risk is genuinely high. These are not failures. They are signals for the next phase.

By day thirty, the organisation should feel different.

Not faster in a dramatic sense. Clearer.

Decisions know where to go. Meetings know why they exist. Reports know what they are for. Leaders are less involved without being less informed.

This is the foundation.

Without a decision architecture reset, any attempt to redesign systems or staffing will be distorted by misrouted authority. Effort will continue to compensate. Load will continue to concentrate.

With it, the organisation becomes receptive to deeper change.

The key outcome of this phase is confidence.

Not confidence that everything is fixed.

Confidence that decisions can move without constant intervention.

That confidence is what allows the organisation to move into the next phase without reverting to firefighting.

Because once decisions flow correctly, structure can finally begin to carry weight.

And leaders can stop acting as the system itself.

Days 31 to 60, Systemisation and Staffability as the First Load-Bearing Moves

By this stage, the organisation has stopped bleeding and decisions are moving with less friction.

What follows is not optimisation. It is reinforcement.

The goal of days thirty one to sixty is to remove human glue and replace it with structure, without triggering panic, disruption, or unnecessary hiring. This is where load is shifted off people and into design for the first time.

The first move is systemisation.

Systemisation here does not mean documentation for its own sake. It means identifying where the organisation is relying on memory, heroics, or informal coordination to function, and replacing that reliance with repeatable flow.

Human glue is easiest to spot now.

It sits where the same people are always involved. Where work only moves when someone chases it. Where outcomes depend on knowing who to speak to rather than on following a defined path.

These areas are not broken. They are overloaded.

The systemisation move is selective. Leaders do not attempt to systemise everything. They focus only on areas carrying disproportionate load. Decision handoffs. Core delivery processes. High volume interactions.

The test is simple.

If this person stepped away for two weeks, what would stall.

Where the answer is unclear, structure is missing.

Systemisation replaces reliance with clarity. It defines sequence. It establishes ownership. It makes the next step obvious without escalation. Importantly, it does not attempt to capture every edge case.

Systems are designed for the eighty percent, not the exception.

This immediately reduces cognitive load. People stop holding context in their heads. Work progresses without constant coordination. Leaders notice fewer interruptions because the system is now doing some of the work they were doing personally.

The second move is staffability.

Staffability is not about adding people. It is about matching roles to the work the system now requires.

As systemisation begins, misalignment becomes visible.

Some roles were defined around firefighting rather than flow. Some individuals were promoted into ambiguity. Some managers have responsibility without the authority or capability to carry it.

The instinct at this point is to hire.

That instinct is resisted.

Before headcount is added, roles are clarified. Expectations are tightened. Authority is made explicit. People are assessed against the redesigned role, not the legacy one.

This often reveals surplus capability in unexpected places.

Strong people who were compensating for weak systems suddenly have capacity. Others who appeared stretched were carrying work that no longer exists once structure is in place.

Seat alignment follows.

Seat alignment is not judgement. It is fit.

Some people thrive once clarity exists. Others struggle because ambiguity was masking capability gaps. This is not failure. It is exposure.

The organisation responds with targeted capability upgrade.

Training is specific. It is tied to decision rights, not generic development. Coaching focuses on judgement within clear boundaries, not confidence building. Support is practical, not motivational.

This avoids headcount panic.

When organisations skip this step, they hire to relieve pressure without removing its cause. Complexity increases. Load returns. Leaders become disappointed that investment did not deliver relief.

Here, pressure is reduced first. Then capability is upgraded to match the new structure.

The third move is protecting leadership bandwidth.

As systemisation and staffability progress, leaders resist the temptation to reinsert themselves. It is common at this stage for leaders to feel unnecessary. That discomfort is a signal that load is shifting correctly.

Leaders observe without intervening.

They allow the system to operate imperfectly. They tolerate small inefficiencies in order to see where design still needs reinforcement. They resist rescuing behaviour that would recreate dependency.

This restraint is essential.

If leaders step back in too early, human glue reforms around them. The organisation reverts. The opportunity is lost.

By the end of sixty days, the organisation should not feel transformed.

It should feel lighter.

Meetings reduce organically because less coordination is required. Decisions resolve without escalation. Certain individuals no longer appear everywhere. Leaders regain time without losing control.

Most importantly, the organisation begins to demonstrate transferability in small ways.

Work continues when someone is absent. Progress does not stall when attention shifts. Outcomes are produced through structure rather than effort.

This phase lays the first load bearing elements.

Systemisation removes reliance on memory.

Staffability ensures roles can carry what the system now demands.

Capability is upgraded without adding weight.

Nothing here is cosmetic.

These moves are quiet, structural, and cumulative. They do not announce greatness. They make it possible.

If this phase is rushed, the organisation adds systems that people cannot use and roles that cannot decide. If it is skipped, leaders remain the glue.

Done correctly, it marks a turning point.

Not where everything works.

But where the organisation no longer needs to be carried to function.

From here, cadence and scale can be introduced without fear of collapse.

Because the weight is finally being carried where it belongs.

Days 61 to 90, Cadence That Holds Under Pressure

By this stage, structure has begun to carry weight.

Decisions move more cleanly. Systems reduce reliance on memory. Roles are clearer. Leaders are less embedded in execution. What remains vulnerable is not capability, but drift.

Cadence exists to prevent that drift.

Cadence is not meetings. It is rhythm. It is how the organisation renews direction, tests alignment, and corrects early without drama. Without cadence, even well designed structures degrade under pressure. With it, they stabilise.

The purpose of days sixty one to ninety is to install rhythms that protect focus and surface strain before it accumulates.

The first rhythm is weekly.

Weekly cadence is operational, not strategic. Its role is to maintain flow.

A strong weekly rhythm answers three questions only.

What moved.

What stalled.

What must be resolved next.

It is not a reporting forum. It is a constraint review. Work that is flowing is acknowledged briefly and left alone. Attention goes to blockage, dependency, and variance.

This rhythm prevents silent accumulation.

When something stalls, it is noticed quickly. When a decision is missing, it is identified early. When effort begins to rise, it is visible. The organisation does not wait for monthly reviews to discover congestion.

Weekly cadence is short, disciplined, and consistent. It exists to keep work moving without escalation.

When done well, it reduces the need for ad hoc meetings. Flow becomes observable without intervention.

The second rhythm is monthly.

Monthly cadence is directional.

Its role is to test alignment between intent and execution. Not through storytelling, but through evidence.

A strong monthly rhythm examines where effort is being spent relative to stated priorities. It asks whether value creation is tracking as expected and where assumptions are being challenged by reality.

This is where drift is corrected calmly.

If a priority is consuming disproportionate effort, it is questioned. If an initiative is progressing without impact, it is paused or reshaped. If new pressure is emerging, it is acknowledged before it becomes urgent.

Monthly cadence is where leaders intervene structurally rather than tactically.

They do not solve problems. They adjust focus, sequence, and resourcing. They protect the organisation from chasing noise while neglecting signal.

This rhythm prevents strategy from becoming rhetorical.

The third rhythm is quarterly.

Quarterly cadence is architectural.

Its role is not planning in the traditional sense. It is load assessment.

A strong quarterly rhythm examines how the organisation is carrying its weight. Where leadership bandwidth is being consumed. Where decisions are still escalating. Where systems are compensating rather than absorbing.

This is where design is adjusted.

Roles are refined. Authority is clarified further. Systems are reinforced or simplified. Capacity is assessed relative to ambition. The organisation decides what it can carry next without burning people.

Quarterly cadence protects optionality.

It prevents the organisation from committing to growth it cannot support structurally. It ensures that ambition remains matched to capacity.

Importantly, quarterly cadence is where leaders regain altitude together. They step out of flow long enough to see patterns. Not to debate vision, but to observe architecture.

Across all three rhythms, one principle holds.

Cadence is not additive.

These rhythms replace noise. They do not add to it. If cadence increases meeting load, it is misdesigned. Each rhythm should reduce ad hoc coordination by making work and strain visible.

Cadence also changes behaviour.

People stop hoarding issues because they know when and where they will be addressed. Leaders stop intervening reflexively because they trust the rhythm to surface what matters. The organisation becomes calmer under pressure because it expects correction.

This is how cadence holds under pressure.

Not by enforcing discipline, but by normalising adjustment.

Without cadence, organisations rely on vigilance. Leaders watch constantly. Teams compensate. Drift is managed through attention.

With cadence, vigilance is replaced by rhythm. The organisation corrects itself before strain accumulates.

The final discipline in this phase is restraint.

Leaders resist the urge to overengineer cadence. They keep questions few. They avoid expanding scope. They allow the rhythm to mature before adding complexity.

Cadence must be boring to be effective.

Predictable.
Consistent.
Unemotional.

When cadence becomes performative, it fails. When it is quiet and reliable, it protects focus.

By day ninety, the organisation should not feel faster in bursts.

It should feel steadier.

Pressure still exists. Complexity remains. What has changed is how early and how calmly the organisation responds. Drift is noticed while still reversible. Load is adjusted before it concentrates. Leaders remain available for design rather than rescue.

This is what cadence is for.

Not motivation.

Not alignment theatre.

Not control.

Cadence is structural memory.

It reminds the organisation what matters, where strain sits, and when to adjust. It allows greatness to hold under pressure without consuming the people inside it.

Without cadence, even the best architecture erodes.

With it, the organisation stays ahead of its own complexity.

Quietly.
Reliably.
Deliberately.

The Moment the Organisation Feels Lighter

The shift does not arrive with celebration.

There is no announcement, no visible milestone, no sudden surge of energy. In fact, it is easy to miss if one is looking for drama. What changes is subtler and more consequential.

The organisation feels lighter.

This lightness is not the absence of pressure. The work has not reduced. Complexity remains. Markets are still volatile. What has changed is where the weight is being carried.

Speed returns without urgency.

Decisions move again, not because people are pushing harder, but because fewer decisions are waiting. Authority resolves issues where they arise. Escalation slows because it is no longer the default. Progress becomes continuous rather than episodic.

The organisation stops surging and stalling.

Meetings begin to disappear.

Not through cancellation mandates, but through irrelevance. Coordination that once required discussion is now handled by structure. Alignment that once required explanation is embedded. Updates are replaced by movement.

What remains are meetings that decide.

This reduction is felt immediately. Time opens. Attention sharpens. Leaders notice gaps in their calendars that were previously unthinkable. Not because work vanished, but because it no longer needs to be carried conversationally.

Exceptions become rare again.

They still exist, but they regain meaning. When something is escalated, it matters. It signals real deviation rather than routine ambiguity. Leaders engage selectively and decisively.

The organisation stops living in exception mode.

This alone reduces cognitive load. People stop anticipating disruption. Plans hold longer. Confidence increases without bravado.

Accountability becomes clearer.

Ownership no longer needs reinforcement. People know what they are responsible for and what they are not. Decisions do not hover. Work does not circulate endlessly. Progress is visible without supervision.

This clarity is not enforced. It is structural.

Leaders experience a change in how they are needed.

They are consulted less frequently, but more meaningfully. When they are involved, it is for judgement, not throughput. They are no longer asked to confirm what the system should already know.

Their role shifts without instruction.

Middle management feels the change most acutely.

They stop managing up reflexively. They stop buffering ambiguity. Their work moves from translation to execution. This is often accompanied by a quiet sense of relief.

They can finally do the job they were hired to do.

The organisation also becomes more honest.

Because compensation has reduced, signals surface earlier. Small issues are seen while still small. There is less incentive to hide friction because friction is no longer punished with intervention. It is treated as information.

This honesty is stabilising.

Importantly, none of this feels like a transformation.

It feels like friction releasing.

The organisation has not become more ambitious. It has become more capable. Effort now produces leverage instead of exhaustion. Energy is spent on progress rather than preservation.

This is the moment leaders often describe as regaining control.

In truth, they are regaining proportion.

Their involvement matches their role. Their attention is used where it adds the most value. The organisation no longer requires them to be everywhere to function.

This lightness is the proof.

Not of motivation.

Not of culture.

Not of leadership charisma.

Of architecture.

It signals that load has been redistributed correctly. That decisions are flowing. That systems are carrying weight. That people are no longer compensating silently.

The organisation still faces challenges.

The difference is that challenges no longer feel cumulative. They are addressed within structure rather than absorbed by individuals.

This is how greatness becomes tangible.

Not as a feeling of triumph.

But as the quiet absence of unnecessary strain.

When the organisation feels lighter, it is not because the work is easy.

It is because the work is finally being carried by design.

CHAPTER 8
Staying Great, Preventing Drift, Protecting Optionality

Why Greatness Decays, Even When Results Look Good

Greatness does not fail dramatically.

It decays quietly.

This decay rarely coincides with poor results. In fact, it often occurs during periods of sustained performance. Revenue holds. Customers remain loyal. Leaders feel validated. The organisation appears stable.

This is precisely when decay begins.

Success recreates complexity.

Every success adds weight. New customers introduce variation. New products create interfaces. New markets add regulatory, cultural, and operational layers. What once fit cleanly now requires coordination.

None of this is negative. It is the cost of growth.

The danger is not complexity itself, but how it accumulates. Complexity compounds faster than organisations redesign. Each success adds structural demand that must be carried. If architecture does not evolve at the same rate, compensation begins again.

The organisation adapts through effort.

People step in. Leaders intervene. Systems are stretched. Results continue. Complexity is absorbed informally rather than structurally. The organisation appears resilient.

In reality, it is returning to dependence.

Success also recreates confidence.

Confidence is earned and deserved. It reinforces judgement. It reduces hesitation. Leaders trust what has worked. The organisation moves decisively.

Over time, confidence hardens into assumption.

Signals that do not fit the established narrative are discounted. Friction is explained away. Early signs of drift are rationalised because outcomes remain strong. Leaders believe they will act when needed.

This belief delays redesign.

Confidence shortens diagnostic patience. Leaders move quickly to solution. They rely on familiar tools. They optimise rather than interrogate. The organisation responds, but architecture remains untouched.

Success validates behaviour, not design.

The third element success recreates is delay.

When results are good, urgency feels unnecessary. Change can wait. Redesign is postponed in favour of execution. Leaders protect momentum by avoiding disruption.

Delay feels responsible.

What is missed is that optionality is time sensitive. The longer redesign is postponed, the more dependencies form. Workarounds harden. Informal authority becomes normal. The cost of change rises quietly.

By the time pain is visible, the organisation has already lost flexibility.

This is the hidden cycle.

Success increases complexity.
Complexity is absorbed through effort.
Effort masks structural strain.
Results remain strong.
Confidence increases.
Redesign is delayed.
Optionality shrinks.
The cycle repeats.

Each turn of the cycle makes the organisation heavier.

Because results hold, the cycle is rarely questioned. Leaders attribute strain to growth. They celebrate resilience. They invest in people and tools. The system continues to function.

Until it does not.

The most dangerous phase is not decline. It is prolonged stability under increasing effort.

This is where greatness erodes.

Not because leaders make poor decisions, but because success suppresses the signals that would justify redesign. The organisation becomes less sensitive to strain. It normalises load that should have triggered change earlier.

Preventing decay requires a different discipline.

Not vigilance in the traditional sense, but structural humility.

Leaders must assume that success is already recreating the conditions for future fragility. That complexity is accumulating even when outcomes are positive. That confidence can blind as easily as it empowers.

This does not require pessimism.

It requires cadence.

Great organisations remain great by continually testing whether their architecture still matches their reality. They do not wait for performance to falter. They measure strain, not just results. They observe where effort is rising and ask why.

They treat redesign as ongoing, not episodic.

This protects optionality.

When architecture is adjusted early, change is calm. Authority can be redistributed without disruption. Systems can be simplified before they ossify. Leaders can step back without destabilising flow.

When redesign is delayed, change becomes corrective. Options narrow. Trade offs harden. Leaders are forced to act from inside pressure rather than ahead of it.

The difference is timing, not insight.

Staying great is not about defending success. It is about recognising what success is doing to the system.

Great organisations accept that decay is not a failure mode. It is a natural outcome of growth without redesign. They do not assume immunity. They build detection into their rhythm.

They watch for early drift.
They test transferability regularly.
They monitor decision congestion.
They observe leadership load.

These are not metrics. They are signals.

When signals appear, they act quietly. They redesign before effort becomes dependence. They protect optionality by intervening while choice still exists.

This is how greatness is sustained.

Not through constant transformation.

Not through heroic leadership.

Not through cultural reinforcement alone.

Through disciplined attention to architecture as success unfolds.

The paradox is simple.

The more successful the organisation becomes, the more deliberately it must question whether that success is being carried structurally or personally.

Those that do remain great.

Those that do not often look fine right up until the moment they are not.

By then, the cycle has already completed.

And optionality has already been spent.

The Drift Prevention System, Signals, Cadence, Enforcement

Drift cannot be eliminated.

It can only be detected early or paid for later.

The organisations that stay great do not attempt to prevent change. They prevent blindness. They design a system that makes early strain visible and forces response before compensation becomes dependence.

This system has three components only.

Signals.
Cadence.
Enforcement.

Anything more becomes noise. Anything less becomes hope.

The first component is signals.

Most organisations track too much and see too little. Dashboards expand while clarity shrinks. The drift prevention system relies on a small number of signals that reveal structural strain regardless of performance.

The first signal is decision latency.

Not how good decisions are, but how long they take relative to context. When decision time increases without a corresponding increase in risk, drift has begun. Latency indicates unclear authority, poor sequence, or rising congestion.

This signal matters because it precedes every other form of slowdown.

The second signal is escalation density.

Not the number of escalations, but their distribution. When similar issues escalate repeatedly, structure is missing. When escalation spreads upward rather than outward, leadership is absorbing load again.

Escalation density shows where authority design is failing.

The third signal is meeting multiplication.

Not total meeting hours, but purpose duplication. When multiple forums exist to resolve the same class of issue, flow has broken. Meetings have become load bearing.

This signal appears long before productivity declines.

The fourth signal is hero dependency.

When specific individuals are consistently required to unblock work, attend exceptions, or maintain momentum, transferability is eroding. The organisation is compensating through people again.

Hero dependency is the most dangerous signal because it is often praised.

The fifth signal is effort to outcome ratio.

When outcomes remain stable but effort increases, drift is already present. People work harder to hold the same line. Coordination rises. Attention fragments.

This signal reveals structural debt accumulating quietly.

These signals are deliberately few.

They do not describe performance. They describe strain. They are observable without surveys, sentiment analysis, or cultural interpretation. Leaders already feel them. The system simply gives them language and focus.

Signals alone are insufficient.

They must be reviewed through cadence.

Cadence is what keeps signals visible when results are still good.

Without cadence, signals are noticed but deferred. Leaders see them, acknowledge them, and move on. Performance reassures. Drift continues.

The drift prevention cadence operates at three levels.

Weekly cadence observes movement.

It asks whether decisions are slowing, whether escalations are rising, whether meetings are increasing. It does not analyse causes deeply. It flags variance.

This keeps small shifts from being normalised.

Monthly cadence interprets patterns.

It looks across weeks to see whether strain is persistent or episodic. It examines where load is moving and whether previous adjustments held. It connects signals rather than reacting to them individually.

This is where early redesign decisions are made.

Quarterly cadence enforces correction.

It reviews whether architecture has been adjusted in response to sustained signals. It tests whether leadership load has reduced or quietly returned. It asks whether transferability has improved or weakened.

Quarterly cadence is where drift is either arrested or allowed to compound.

The final component is enforcement.

This is the element most organisations avoid.

Enforcement is not control. It is consequence.

Without enforcement, signals become interesting but optional. Cadence becomes ritual. Drift resumes.

Enforcement means agreeing in advance what will happen when signals persist.

If decision latency increases for two consecutive cycles, authority design is reviewed.

If escalation density rises, escalation paths are redesigned.

If meetings multiply, forums are removed before new ones are added.

If hero dependency reappears, load is deliberately extracted from individuals and redesigned structurally.

These responses are not debated each time. They are predefined.

This removes emotion.

Leaders do not argue about whether intervention is necessary. The system already decided. The response is mechanical, not personal.

This is why enforcement protects optionality.

It ensures that redesign happens while choice still exists. It prevents leaders from deferring action because performance remains acceptable. It stops confidence from overriding evidence.

Importantly, enforcement applies to leaders first.

If leadership calendars refill, if leaders reinsert themselves into throughput, if decisions reconcentrate, the system flags this as drift, not dedication.

This requires discipline.

Leaders must allow themselves to be constrained by the system they designed. Without this, drift prevention collapses into aspiration.

The drift prevention system is intentionally unsentimental.

It does not care how hard people are working.

It does not reward heroics.

It does not wait for pain.

It observes strain.

It surfaces patterns.

It forces response.

This is how greatness is protected.

Not through constant vigilance.

Not through cultural reinforcement.

Not through periodic transformation.

Through a small set of signals reviewed rhythmically and acted on without debate.

The paradox is that once this system is in place, it rarely needs to be used aggressively.

Because drift is corrected early, quietly, and proportionately.

The organisation stays light not because it is perfect, but because it refuses to let compensation become normal again.

This is the difference between organisations that remain great and those that slowly give their greatness back.

One watches results.

The other watches strain.

Only one protects optionality over time.

AI as a Force Multiplier, Not a Crutch

AI does not change what an organisation is.

It amplifies it.

This is the first mistake leaders make when introducing AI. They treat it as capability rather than acceleration. As solution rather than stress test. AI does not fix weak architecture. It exposes it faster.

Where structure is sound, AI multiplies leverage.

Where structure is weak, AI multiplies error.

Understanding this distinction determines whether AI strengthens the organisation or accelerates its decay.

AI strengthens architecture when direction is clear.

AI is exceptionally good at speed, pattern recognition, and repetition. It can analyse, recommend, and execute faster than human teams. What it cannot do is decide what matters.

When direction is structurally clear, AI becomes a powerful amplifier. It prioritises correctly. It allocates effort efficiently. It reinforces intent because the system it operates within already knows where to go.

When direction is vague, AI accelerates drift.

It optimises locally. It pursues conflicting objectives simultaneously. It produces volume without coherence. Leaders receive more output, not more clarity.

AI does not create confusion. It operationalises it.

This is why organisations that introduce AI without architectural clarity often feel busier but not better. Activity increases. Insight proliferates. Decisions do not improve.

The problem is not the technology. It is the absence of a directional spine.

AI strengthens architecture when value flows.

In organisations with clear process flow and decision rights, AI reduces friction. It removes manual coordination. It shortens cycles. It increases predictability.

Work moves faster because AI is removing effort from places where structure already exists.

In organisations with broken flow, AI increases noise.

It generates insights that cannot be acted on. It produces recommendations that require escalation. It highlights problems faster than the organisation can resolve them. Pressure rises.

Leaders mistake this for complexity created by AI.

In reality, AI is revealing how little of the organisation's work was ever designed to move cleanly.

AI cannot compensate for missing flow. It only makes its absence more obvious.

AI strengthens architecture when movement is structured.

Where initiatives progress through defined stages with clear ownership, AI accelerates execution. It supports planning. It monitors variance. It flags constraint early.

Where movement depends on intervention, AI creates bottlenecks.

It produces more work than leaders can absorb. It surfaces more exceptions than the organisation can handle. It increases demand for judgement without increasing capacity for it.

AI does not reduce leadership load by default. It redistributes it.

If leadership was already the bottleneck, AI makes that visible faster.

This is why AI often disappoints senior teams.

They expect leverage and receive overload.

The issue is not adoption. It is placement.

AI should be applied where decisions are already routable, where authority is clear, and where outcomes are defined. Applied elsewhere, it accelerates escalation and concentrates load.

AI also accelerates mistakes.

This is uncomfortable, but necessary.

Where incentives are misaligned, AI optimises the wrong things efficiently.

Where data reflects historical bias, AI reinforces it quickly.

Where metrics are flawed, AI makes them more influential.

The organisation does not get smarter. It gets faster at doing what it was already doing.

This is why AI must follow architecture, not precede it.

Introducing AI into a compensating system increases dependence. People rely on outputs they do not fully understand. Judgement is deferred. Errors propagate before being noticed.

In a designed system, AI is constrained by structure.

In an undesigned system, AI becomes another source of drift.

This is also where leaders misuse AI as a crutch.

They deploy AI to reduce workload rather than redesign load.

They expect automation to replace clarity.

They hope tools will fix congestion.

AI cannot resolve ambiguity.

It can only operate within it.

Used correctly, AI removes friction from well designed processes. Used incorrectly, it creates the illusion of progress while deepening architectural debt.

The correct posture toward AI is therefore restrained.

AI is introduced after decision architecture is clear.

AI is applied where flow already exists.

AI is monitored for where it increases escalation.

AI is constrained by cadence and enforcement.

In this posture, AI becomes a force multiplier.

It shortens cycles without distorting priorities.

It increases throughput without increasing leadership load.

It enhances transferability by embedding knowledge into systems rather than people.

In the wrong posture, AI becomes a force accelerator.

It accelerates drift.

It accelerates dependency.

It accelerates exhaustion.

The difference is not sophistication. It is sequencing.

Organisations that succeed with AI do not ask what AI can do. They ask where the organisation is structurally ready to absorb acceleration.

This is why AI adoption is an architectural decision, not a technical one.

It tests whether the organisation has:

Clear direction that can be operationalised.

Defined value flow that can be accelerated.

Structured movement that can absorb speed.

Decision rights that can handle increased volume.

Without these, AI increases strain.

With them, AI increases leverage.

This chapter is not a warning against AI.

It is a warning against treating AI as a substitute for design.

AI will not save organisations from architectural weakness.

It will reveal it sooner.

Leaders who understand this do not rush adoption. They sequence it. They redesign first, then accelerate.

Those who do not often feel impressed early and overwhelmed later.

AI is not the future of greatness.

Architecture is.

AI simply ensures that the gap between the two closes faster, one way or the other.

Building Transferability, The Final Proof

Transferability is not an initiative.

It is an outcome.

When organisations talk about succession, delegation, or documentation, they often treat them as programmes to be implemented. In reality, these are tests. They reveal whether the organisation is being carried by design or by individuals.

Transferability is the final proof because it cannot be simulated.

If the organisation performs only when specific people are present, it is not yet built. It is being carried.

Succession exposes this first.

Succession planning usually focuses on people. Who is next. Who is ready. Who could step in. These questions matter, but they miss the structural issue.

In a dependent organisation, succession is always risky, regardless of who follows.

The system requires the judgement, memory, and presence of the person leaving. Authority is informal. Context is tacit. Decisions are routed personally. When that person steps away, the organisation slows or destabilises.

In a transferable organisation, succession is anticlimactic.

The role changes hands. The system holds. Performance continues. This does not mean individuals are interchangeable. It means the organisation is not dependent.

Succession works only when structure precedes people.

Decisions must belong to roles, not personalities.

Context must live in systems, not heads.

Escalation must be designed, not improvised.

Without these elements, succession planning becomes theatre.

Delegation reveals the same truth.

Delegation fails in most organisations not because leaders refuse to let go, but because the organisation cannot carry what is delegated.

Work is handed off without authority.

Responsibility is assigned without decision rights.

Outcomes are expected without support.

Leaders intervene to protect results. Delegation becomes supervision. Supervision becomes exhaustion.

The conclusion is predictable.

Leaders decide delegation is risky. They pull work back. Dependency deepens.

This is not a leadership flaw. It is a design gap.

True delegation requires transferability.

People must know what they can decide.

They must have access to the information required.

They must operate within flow that supports action.

They must be protected from escalation being used as control.

When these conditions exist, delegation stops feeling like risk. It becomes normal.

Leaders step back not through discipline, but through necessity. Their involvement is no longer required for routine progress.

Documentation plays a critical role here, but it is often misunderstood.

Most documentation creates compliance, not flow.

It describes what should happen rather than enabling what does happen. It is written for audit, not for movement. People reference it when challenged, not when acting.

This type of documentation does not create transferability. It creates defensibility.

Documentation that creates flow is different.

It clarifies sequence.

It defines decision points.

It makes ownership obvious.

It removes the need for interpretation.

Flow documentation is used in motion, not after the fact. It reduces questions rather than generating them. It allows work to progress without escalation.

This is why excessive documentation often coincides with low transferability.

The organisation is compensating for missing clarity by recording everything. People comply, but they do not act independently.

Transferable organisations document less, but better.

They document only what must be consistent.

They design for the eighty percent.

They allow judgement at the edges.

This balance is what allows flow without fragility.

Transferability also changes how leaders measure success.

They stop asking whether things worked.

They ask whether things worked without them.

They notice where their absence creates silence or slowdown. They treat that as a design signal, not a loyalty issue. They redesign rather than reinsert themselves.

Over time, their presence becomes additive rather than essential.

This is the moment greatness becomes durable.

Not when performance peaks.

Not when growth accelerates.

But when the organisation continues to function during absence, transition, and pressure.

Transferability is uncomfortable because it removes the leader as hero.

It replaces indispensability with design.

It replaces admiration with continuity.

It replaces effort with capacity.

Some leaders resist this subconsciously. Being needed feels like value. Being unnecessary feels like loss.

In reality, being unnecessary is the highest form of leadership.

It means the organisation carries itself.

It means success is embedded.

It means greatness is no longer fragile.

This is the final proof because it cannot be argued away.

Either work moves without specific people, or it does not.

Either decisions resolve without intervention, or they do not.

Either leadership absence causes disruption, or it does not.

There is no narrative here. Only evidence.

Organisations that reach this point experience a profound shift.

They can scale without fear.

They can change leaders without trauma.

They can adopt new tools without overload.

They can face volatility without reverting to heroics.

They have optionality.

This is what all the previous work was for.

Not elegance.

Not theory.

Not frameworks.

Transferability.

It proves that structure is carrying load.

It proves that effort has been replaced by design.

It proves that greatness is no longer conditional.

Everything before this prepares the ground.

This confirms it.

And once confirmed, it changes how leaders think about their organisation forever.

Because they no longer ask how strong their people are.

They ask whether the organisation can stand without them.

That answer tells them everything they need to know.

CONCLUSION:
Great Is Not a Status, It Is a Structure

Greatness has been treated as an achievement.

A point reached. A label earned. A state to be defended. Organisations become "great" and then focus on staying there through discipline, culture, and effort. Performance is monitored. Standards are reinforced. Success is protected.

This framing is incomplete.

Great is not a status. It is a structure.

Status describes where an organisation is today. Structure determines what it can survive tomorrow. Performance without structure is temporary. Structure without performance is theoretical. Greatness exists only when performance is carried by design rather than by people.

This requires a new definition.

Great is not high performance.

Great is performance that survives pressure.

Pressure exposes whether success is being carried by effort or absorbed by architecture. Under pressure, dependent organisations strain. Leaders intervene. People compensate. Results may hold, but at increasing cost.

In structurally great organisations, pressure reveals capacity. Decisions continue to flow. Priorities remain clear. Leaders retain altitude. The system flexes rather than fractures.

Great is not growth.

Great is growth that survives change.

Change tests transferability. Markets shift. Products evolve. Technology accelerates. Leaders move roles. In dependent organisations, each change requires reassembly. Context is rebuilt. Momentum stalls.

In structurally great organisations, change is disruptive but contained. Authority is clear. Knowledge is embedded. Flow persists. The organisation adapts without starting over.

Great is not leadership strength.

Great is leadership that can leave without collapse.

Leadership transitions are the ultimate audit. When leaders step back, do decisions still resolve. Does work still move. Does the organisation continue to progress.

If performance depends on presence, greatness was never embedded. It was borrowed.

The work of this book has been to make that distinction visible.

From the early plateau after success, through invisible load, decision congestion, and drift, a pattern emerges. Organisations do not fail because they lack ambition or talent. They fail because they outgrow the structures that once carried them.

Effort fills the gap.

Success delays correction.

Confidence defers redesign.

Until optionality narrows.

The alternative is not heroic leadership or constant transformation. It is architectural discipline.

Architectural discipline means accepting that structure, not behaviour, carries weight at scale. That culture amplifies design but cannot replace it. That decisions, not people, are usually the bottleneck. That load always transfers and must be deliberately placed.

Most importantly, it means redefining what leaders are responsible for.

Not being the smartest person in the room.

Not absorbing pressure personally.

Not making every critical decision.

But designing organisations that can.

This redefinition is uncomfortable because it removes familiar sources of value. Leaders who have built success through involvement must learn to create value through absence. Through systems that work without them. Through clarity that does not require reinforcement.

This is not loss. It is elevation.

The new definition of great is therefore precise.

Great is an organisation that:

Performs without exhausting its people.

Decides without escalating routinely.

Adapts without destabilising.

Scales without concentrating risk.

Transitions leadership without losing momentum.

These are not aspirations. They are structural outcomes.

They cannot be achieved through motivation, culture, or intelligence alone. They require deliberate design, ongoing cadence, and enforcement that protects optionality.

The promise of this book has not been inspiration.

It has been inevitability.

If organisations continue to pursue greatness as status, they will drift. If they treat greatness as structure, they will endure.

This distinction matters now more than ever.

Speed, volatility, and AI are compressing timelines. There is less time to compensate. Less margin for heroics. Less tolerance for redesign under crisis. Architecture must carry more weight, sooner.

Leaders who recognise this early act calmly. They redesign while choice exists. They protect capacity before it is consumed. They build organisations that remain great beyond their own tenure.

Leaders who delay are not reckless.

They are human.

They trust what has worked. They protect momentum. They wait for pain to justify change. By the time pain arrives, structure has already been stressed beyond its design limits.

This book has offered a different path.

Not a method.

Not a toolkit.

Not a promise.

A lens.

A way to see what effort hides.

A way to read pressure as information.

A way to measure strength without sentiment.

Greatness, redefined, is no longer a badge.

It is the quiet confidence that the organisation can carry itself through what is coming.

Pressure will arrive.

Change will accelerate.

Leaders will move on.

The only question that matters is whether the organisation was designed for that reality.

If it was, greatness will not need defending.

It will persist.

Because it was never a status to begin with.

It was a structure.

The Choice Leaders Actually Make

Leaders rarely face the choice they believe they are making.

They think the decision is whether to change or stay the course. Whether to disrupt success or protect it. Whether to act now or wait for clearer evidence.

Those are surface choices.

The real choice is simpler and harder to avoid.

Carry the weight longer, or redesign what carries it.

Most leaders choose to carry it longer.

Not because they are reckless. Because the organisation still works. Results still arrive. Customers are still served. The weight feels heavy, but manageable. Carrying it personally appears responsible.

This choice feels safe.

Leaders intervene more. They arbitrate decisions. They hold context. They absorb risk. They protect momentum. The organisation continues to function because someone is compensating.

From the inside, this looks like leadership.

From a structural view, it is load being misplaced.

Carrying the weight longer does not hold the organisation steady. It changes it.

Decision making recentres.

Authority blurs.

Dependency increases.

Transferability weakens.

Each act of compensation solves a problem and teaches the system that compensation will continue. Over time, the organisation stops attempting to carry weight itself. It routes pressure upward by design.

Leaders become essential.

This is why carrying the weight longer always feels temporary and becomes permanent.

The alternative choice is quieter.

Redesign what carries the weight.

This does not feel urgent when results are good. It does not provide immediate relief. It often creates short term friction because compensation is being removed.

This is why it is delayed.

Redesign requires leaders to tolerate visible strain without absorbing it immediately. It requires them to let the system reveal where it cannot cope. It requires patience while clarity forms.

This feels counterintuitive to leaders whose identity is built on resolution.

Yet redesign is the only choice that preserves optionality.

When structure carries load, pressure becomes information rather than threat. Decisions resolve where they belong. Authority aligns with accountability. Leaders regain altitude not by stepping back, but by being made unnecessary for routine flow.

The organisation becomes capable rather than dependent.

The difficulty is that both choices can look identical for a time.

Carrying the weight longer maintains performance.

Redesigning structure may slow things briefly.

From the outside, one looks successful and the other risky.

From the inside, one feels familiar and the other uncomfortable.

Time is the differentiator.

Carrying the weight longer compounds cost invisibly. Leaders become more involved. Decision speed slows. Talent narrows. The organisation adapts around dependency. When change finally forces redesign, it is disruptive and expensive.

Redesigning what carries the weight compounds capacity. Each adjustment reduces future effort. Leaders intervene less without trying to. The organisation becomes lighter under the same pressure.

The cost profiles diverge slowly, then suddenly.

This is why leaders often believe they are choosing between action and patience.

In reality, they are choosing where cost accumulates.

Either cost accumulates in people, attention, and leadership bandwidth.

Or it accumulates once, deliberately, in redesign.

There is no third option.

Choosing to carry the weight longer is not neutral. It is an active choice to spend future optionality to protect present stability.

Choosing to redesign is not aggressive. It is a decision to protect future choice at the expense of short term comfort.

Neither choice is moral.

Both are rational.

One is finite.

Leaders eventually discover that their organisation cannot be carried indefinitely. Volume increases. Complexity compounds. Leadership bandwidth saturates. At that point, redesign is forced rather than chosen.

The only difference is timing.

When redesign is chosen early, it is precise.

When redesign is forced late, it is blunt.

Early redesign reshapes load paths.

Late redesign removes people.

Early redesign preserves culture.

Late redesign tests it.

Early redesign maintains control.

Late redesign occurs under pressure.

This is the inevitability most leaders sense but struggle to articulate.

They are not deciding whether to change.

They are deciding whether to keep paying the cost personally or to move the cost into structure where it belongs.

The moment this is seen clearly, the debate ends.

There is no persuasion required.

Leaders recognise that carrying the weight longer does not make them indispensable. It makes the organisation fragile. Redesigning what carries the weight does not diminish leadership. It completes it.

This is the choice leaders actually make.

Not today versus tomorrow.

Not stability versus growth.

Not tradition versus innovation.

Effort versus design.

Dependence versus transferability.

Carrying versus building.

The organisation will continue either way.

The only question is who or what will be carrying it.

And for how long.

A Final Warning, The Cost of Delay

Delay feels harmless because it is incremental.

No single moment marks the loss. No decision announces the narrowing of choice. Leaders continue to operate with the same intelligence, discipline, and intent that created success. The organisation still performs. The system still functions.

Optionality shrinks anyway.

This is the danger of delay. It does not remove options immediately. It quietly prices them out.

In the early stages of strain, intervention is cheap.

Authority can be clarified without disruption. Systems can be simplified without resistance. Roles can be realigned without threatening identity. Leaders can step back gradually. The organisation adjusts with minimal noise because it has not yet adapted around compensation.

At this stage, redesign feels calm.

Delay pushes intervention into a different category.

As time passes, the organisation reorganises itself around workarounds. Informal authority hardens. Dependencies become normal. People are promoted because they compensate well, not because roles are clear. Systems are layered to manage exceptions rather than remove them.

What was once flexible becomes fixed.

Optionality shrinks because every workaround creates a constituency. Every exception builds reliance. Every act of compensation trains the organisation to route load away from structure and into people.

By the time leaders feel compelled to act, the cost profile has changed.

Redesign now disrupts livelihoods.

Clarifying authority threatens status.

Removing dependencies feels like removing safety.

Simplifying systems looks like regression.

The same changes that would have been absorbed earlier now provoke resistance.

This is not political. It is structural.

The organisation has learned to survive through compensation. Removing that compensation feels like danger. People defend what allows them to function, even if it is inefficient.

Delay also changes where cost is paid.

Early intervention concentrates cost in design effort.

Late intervention concentrates cost in people.

When redesign is delayed, the organisation eventually pays through burnout, attrition, stalled growth, or forced restructuring. Leaders are surprised by the severity of the response because the preceding drift felt manageable.

It was not manageable. It was cumulative.

Optionality does not disappear all at once. It decays.

Each month of delay reduces sequencing flexibility.

Each quarter of delay increases dependency.

Each year of delay hardens architecture around compensation.

The rebuild becomes heavier not because the organisation grew, but because it adapted incorrectly.

This is why late intervention is always more expensive.

It requires unlearning as well as redesign.

It requires breaking habits as well as building structure.

It requires decisive action under pressure rather than deliberate action under choice.

Leaders often tell themselves they are buying time.

They are not.

They are converting time into debt.

Structural debt behaves differently from financial debt. It does not demand repayment on schedule. It charges interest in effort, coordination, and leadership bandwidth. The interest is paid daily and unnoticed.

The principal is called due without warning.

When that moment arrives, leaders act quickly and forcefully. They remove layers. They replace people. They centralise decisions. They stabilise through control.

This works briefly.

It does not restore optionality. It consumes what remains.

The earlier the intervention, the cheaper the rebuild because less must be undone.

Design changes are additive rather than corrective.

Authority can be clarified without confrontation.

Systems can be simplified without loss of face.

Leaders can withdraw without creating vacuum.

Later, every change is subtractive.

Something must be taken away.

Someone must lose influence.

Some dependency must be broken.

This is why early redesign feels thoughtful and late redesign feels brutal.

The warning here is not emotional.

It is mathematical.

The cost of change increases as a function of delay because compensation compounds faster than capacity. The longer the organisation relies on effort, the more structure ossifies around it.

Leaders cannot reverse this through intent.

They can only choose when to stop allowing it.

This is the final reality.

There is no moment where delay becomes free again.

There is no plateau where optionality stabilises.

There is no equilibrium where compensation stops accumulating cost.

Waiting does not hold position. It moves the organisation closer to a point where redesign is no longer elective.

The warning is therefore simple.

Intervene while clarity is available, not when pain demands it. Redesign while options exist, not when they have narrowed. Move load into structure while leaders still have space, not when they are exhausted.

This is not urgency. It is accuracy.

Leaders who act early do not look dramatic. They look measured. They redesign quietly. They protect capacity before it is consumed. They preserve choice.

Leaders who delay are not negligent. They are human. They trust success. They wait for certainty. They act when pressure justifies it.

By then, the rebuild is heavier than it needed to be.

Optionality has a half life.

Every period of delay reduces what can be done calmly, cheaply, and precisely. The organisation will still change. That is inevitable.

The only variable is whether change occurs while the organisation still has room to choose how.

This is the cost of delay.

It is not failure.

It is not collapse.

It is not incompetence.

It is the silent conversion of choice into necessity.

And once that conversion is complete, no amount of leadership effort can buy it back.

A Final Warning, The Cost of Delay

Delay feels harmless because it is incremental.

No single moment marks the loss. No decision announces the narrowing of choice. Leaders continue to operate with the same intelligence, discipline, and intent that created success. The organisation still performs. The system still functions.

Optionality shrinks anyway.

This is the danger of delay. It does not remove options immediately. It quietly prices them out.

In the early stages of strain, intervention is cheap.

Authority can be clarified without disruption. Systems can be simplified without resistance. Roles can be realigned without threatening identity. Leaders can step back gradually. The organisation adjusts with minimal noise because it has not yet adapted around compensation.

At this stage, redesign feels calm.

Delay pushes intervention into a different category.

As time passes, the organisation reorganises itself around workarounds. Informal authority hardens. Dependencies become normal. People are promoted because they compensate well, not because roles are clear. Systems are layered to manage exceptions rather than remove them.

What was once flexible becomes fixed.

Optionality shrinks because every workaround creates a constituency. Every exception builds reliance. Every act of compensation trains the organisation to route load away from structure and into people.

By the time leaders feel compelled to act, the cost profile has changed.

Redesign now disrupts livelihoods.

Clarifying authority threatens status.

Removing dependencies feels like removing safety.

Simplifying systems looks like regression.

The same changes that would have been absorbed earlier now provoke resistance.

This is not political. It is structural.

The organisation has learned to survive through compensation. Removing that compensation feels like danger. People defend what allows them to function, even if it is inefficient.

Delay also changes where cost is paid.

Early intervention concentrates cost in design effort.

Late intervention concentrates cost in people.

When redesign is delayed, the organisation eventually pays through burnout, attrition, stalled growth, or forced restructuring. Leaders are surprised by the severity of the response because the preceding drift felt manageable.

It was not manageable. It was cumulative.

Optionality does not disappear all at once. It decays.

Each month of delay reduces sequencing flexibility.

Each quarter of delay increases dependency.

Each year of delay hardens architecture around compensation.

The rebuild becomes heavier not because the organisation grew, but because it adapted incorrectly.

This is why late intervention is always more expensive.

It requires unlearning as well as redesign.

It requires breaking habits as well as building structure.

It requires decisive action under pressure rather than deliberate action under choice.

Leaders often tell themselves they are buying time.

They are not.

They are converting time into debt.

Structural debt behaves differently from financial debt. It does not demand repayment on schedule. It charges interest in effort, coordination, and leadership bandwidth. The interest is paid daily and unnoticed.

The principal is called due without warning.

When that moment arrives, leaders act quickly and forcefully. They remove layers. They replace people. They centralise decisions. They stabilise through control.

This works briefly.

It does not restore optionality. It consumes what remains.

The earlier the intervention, the cheaper the rebuild because less must be undone.

Design changes are additive rather than corrective.

Authority can be clarified without confrontation.

Systems can be simplified without loss of face.

Leaders can withdraw without creating vacuum.

Later, every change is subtractive.

Something must be taken away.

Someone must lose influence.

Some dependency must be broken.

This is why early redesign feels thoughtful and late redesign feels brutal.

The warning here is not emotional.

It is mathematical.

The cost of change increases as a function of delay because compensation compounds faster than capacity. The longer the organisation relies on effort, the more structure ossifies around it.

Leaders cannot reverse this through intent.

They can only choose when to stop allowing it.

This is the final reality.

There is no moment where delay becomes free again.

There is no plateau where optionality stabilises.

There is no equilibrium where compensation stops accumulating cost.

Waiting does not hold position. It moves the organisation closer to a point where redesign is no longer elective.

The warning is therefore simple.

Intervene while clarity is available, not when pain demands it.

Redesign while options exist, not when they have narrowed.

Move load into structure while leaders still have space, not when they are exhausted.

This is not urgency. It is accuracy.

Leaders who act early do not look dramatic. They look measured. They redesign quietly. They protect capacity before it is consumed. They preserve choice.

Leaders who delay are not negligent. They are human. They trust success. They wait for certainty. They act when pressure justifies it.

By then, the rebuild is heavier than it needed to be.

Optionality has a half life.

Every period of delay reduces what can be done calmly, cheaply, and precisely. The organisation will still change. That is inevitable.

The only variable is whether change occurs while the organisation still has room to choose how.

This is the cost of delay.

It is not failure.

It is not collapse.

It is not incompetence.

It is the silent conversion of choice into necessity.

And once that conversion is complete, no amount of leadership effort can buy it back.

A Note from the Author

If this book challenged your thinking, unsettled a comfortable assumption, or helped you see your organisation more clearly, I ask one simple favour: please leave an honest review on Amazon.

Reviews matter far more than most readers realise. They are not about praise or promotion. They are how serious books reach the right audience and avoid the wrong one. Thoughtful reviews help other leaders decide whether this book is for them, or whether it is not, before they invest their time.

I do not expect agreement. In fact, disagreement is often a sign the book has done its job. What matters is accuracy, clarity, and truth from your perspective as a reader.

This work was written for leaders carrying real weight and real consequence. Your review helps ensure it reaches those people, and spares others who are looking for something different.

Thank you for reading, and for taking a moment to share your perspective.

Moe Nawaz

www.ingramcontent.com/pod-product-compliance
Lightning Source LLC
Chambersburg PA
CBHW052155220526
45471CB00004B/1683